"For over twenty years, [...] had a front-row seat to the messy, slow process of sanctification in the lives of the saints. I have witnessed the miraculous breakthrough where addiction or anger seems to supernaturally lift and never return, but I intentionally used the words *miraculous* and *supernatural* because I have watched hundreds of people surrender to Jesus, love him, and have a hard time breaking free of certain indwelling sins. I'm grateful for books like Jon's. It reads like real life to me: grimy, hard . . . honest. The Lord is faithful to deliver us. *Confessions of a Christian Alcoholic* is a testimony to that faithfulness."

Matt Chandler, lead pastor of The Village Church

"This book tackles the 'quiet part out loud' that so many of us sitting in the pew on Sundays wished someone would talk about on a Monday morning . . . or better yet, a Friday night! No matter if you're questioning your drinking habits in this alcohol-centric society or if you know it's something that needs to change—this book is for you."

Jenn Kautsch, author of *Look Alive, Sis* and founder of the SoberSis community

"We think Christian and alcoholic are two identities that shouldn't (couldn't?) be mingled. And yet, if we're honest, isn't that all too common within the church—a believer in public while struggling in private? Jon just had the courage to state it with a refreshingly raw combination of boldness, humility, and transformation. *Confessions of a Christian Alcoholic* exposes an ailment of the church: Once we confess Christ, we cease confessing sin . . . and to be silent with sin is to be ensnared by sin. Jon gives us Jesus, who both saves us and keeps us safe."

John Elmore (nineteen years sober), local pastor of Harris Creek (Waco, TX); author of *Freedom Starts Today*

"*Confessions of a Christian Alcoholic* is a book we all need. Even if your struggle isn't with alcohol, this book is for you—because, in some way, we're all addicts. This is a must-read for anyone seeking grace amid their brokenness—whatever form it takes."

Tullian Tchividjian, author of *Carnage & Grace*

"As a neurosurgeon, I'm in the business of trying to save lives. And when I find something to help me do that, I prescribe it to everyone who needs it. Jon Seidl has written such a prescription in *Confessions of a Christian Alcoholic*. It could have been titled *Confessions of a Christian* because Jon's words apply to everyone who has chosen a surrogate with which to anesthetize themselves from the sin and shame life so often brings. His radical call not just to come to Jesus but to become like Jesus is the medicine we all so desperately need no matter what we're struggling with."

W. Lee Warren, MD, neurosurgeon, author of *Hope Is the First Dose*, and host of *The Self-Brain Surgery Podcast with Dr. Lee Warren*

"Praise God for *Confessions of a Christian Alcoholic*! Dripping with honesty and vulnerability, it's a special reminder that sanctification is an ongoing process that is never done this side of heaven. In fact, sin is creeping outside all our doors, and Christians are not immune from falling prey to the devil's tactics. All Christians—not just those struggling with addictive behaviors or misordered loves—will benefit from this book's gospel truths, deep wisdom, and important takeaways. As someone who has had a front-row seat to Jon's 'messy sanctification' story over the last couple years, I thank God for his work in Jon's life and am excited to see the impact this book will have."

Afshin Ziafat, lead pastor of Providence Church; board member of The Gospel Coalition

"*Confessions of a Christian Alcoholic* is an honest and redemptive work that courageously illuminates the intersection of faith, addiction, and trauma. Jon's bold commitment to vulnerability and healing is inspiring. His words offer hope for those struggling with the wounds that often fuel addiction, and he offers practical wisdom grounded in the transformative power of Christ's love. *Confessions* is a guide for anyone longing to break free and embrace the messy, beautiful process of healing."

Gina Birkemeier, LPC, author of Generations Deep

"*Confessions of a Christian Alcoholic* is the kind of book the church desperately needs—one that doesn't shy away from the messiness of real-life struggles, especially addiction struggles that countless Christians battle in shamed silence. Instead, it meets them with raw honesty and deep hope. Jon's vulnerability is a gift, reminding us that healing isn't about perfection but about surrender. If you've ever wrestled with shame, addiction, or the fear of being 'too broken,' this book will be a lifeline. A must-read for anyone seeking freedom and true transformation."

Dr. Zoe Shaw, psychotherapist, author, and host of Stronger in the Difficult Places

"*Confessions of a Christian Alcoholic* is the book we've needed in the faith community for years. Jon's raw honesty and powerful words speak to the heart of the matter and what it means to wrestle with our deepest struggles in a broken world. This book is a must-read for any Christian who has ever struggled with alcohol dependence in any way."

Ericka Andersen, journalist and author of the forthcoming book Freely Sober

CONFESSIONS
OF A CHRISTIAN
ALCOHOLIC

CONFESSIONS OF A CHRISTIAN ALCOHOLIC

A Candid Conversation on Drinking, Addiction, and How to Break Free

Jonathon M. Seidl

a division of Baker Publishing Group
Grand Rapids, Michigan

© 2025 by Jonathon M. Seidl

Published by Revell
a division of Baker Publishing Group
Grand Rapids, Michigan
RevellBooks.com

Printed in the United States of America

All rights reserved. No part of this publication may be reproduced, stored in a retrieval system, or transmitted in any form or by any means—for example, electronic, photocopy, recording—without the prior written permission of the publisher. The only exception is brief quotations in printed reviews.

Library of Congress Cataloging-in-Publication Data
Names: Seidl, Jonathon M., 1987– author.
Title: Confessions of a Christian alcoholic : a candid conversation on drinking, addiction, and how to break free / Jonathon M. Seidl.
Description: Grand Rapids, Michigan : Revell, a division of Baker Publishing Group, [2025] | Includes bibliographical references.
Identifiers: LCCN 2024060318 | ISBN 9780800747305 (paperback) | ISBN 9780800747510 (casebound) | ISBN 9781493451548 (ebook)
Subjects: LCSH: Seidl, Jonathon M., 1987– | Alcoholics—United States—Biography. | Alcoholics—Religious life. | Alcoholism—Religious aspects—Christianity. | Drinking of alcoholic beverages—Religious aspects—Christianity. | LCGFT: Autobiographies.
Classification: LCC BV4596.A48 S45 2025 | DDC 362.292092 [B]—dc23/eng/20250216
LC record available at https://lccn.loc.gov/2024060318

Unless otherwise indicated, Scripture quotations are from The Holy Bible, English Standard Version® (ESV®). Copyright © 2001 by Crossway, a publishing ministry of Good News Publishers. Used by permission. All rights reserved. ESV Text Edition: 2016

Scripture quotations labeled MSG are from *The Message*. Copyright © 1993, 2002, 2018 by Eugene H. Peterson. Used by permission of NavPress. All rights reserved. Represented by Tyndale House Publishers.

Scripture quotations labeled NIV are from the Holy Bible, New International Version®, NIV®. Copyright © 1973, 1978, 1984, 2011 by Biblica, Inc.® Used by permission of Zondervan. All rights reserved worldwide. www.zondervan.com. The "NIV" and "New International Version" are trademarks registered in the United States Patent and Trademark Office by Biblica, Inc.®

Extracts from *The Screwtape Letters* by C. S. Lewis, copyright ©1942 C. S. Lewis Pte. Ltd., reprinted by permission.

Extracts from *The Great Divorce* by C. S. Lewis, copyright ©1946 C. S. Lewis Pte. Ltd., reprinted by permission.

Cover design and illustration by Chris Kuhatschek.

This publication is intended to provide helpful and informative material on the subjects addressed. The author and publisher expressly disclaim responsibility for any adverse effects arising from the use or application of the information contained in this book. This book is not intended as a guide to diagnose or treat medical or psychological problems. If medical, psychological, or other expert assistance is required, the reader should seek the services of a healthcare provider or certified counselor.

The names and details of the people and situations described in this book have been used with permission. To protect the privacy of individuals, some names and identifying details have been changed.

The author is represented by the literary agency of A Drop of Ink, LLC, www.adropofink.pub.

Baker Publishing Group publications use paper produced from sustainable forestry practices and postconsumer waste whenever possible.

25 26 27 28 29 30 31   7 6 5 4 3 2 1

To Brett, Annie, and Jack.
By aiming for more of Jesus, I also got more of you.
It's a grace I do not deserve.

Contents

Preface 13
Introduction: Blitzed on the Beach 17

Part 1: My Story
1. Drunk at Deer Camp 41
2. Am I an Alcoholic? 47
3. A Slow Fade 66

Part 2: Making Sense of It
4. How Does This Happen? 93
5. Root vs. Fruit 114
6. Combating Shame 134
7. Messy Sanctification 148

Part 3: Breaking Free

   8. Finding Sobriety   167

   9. Abiding in Christ (Step 1)   182

  10. Finding Your True Identity (Step 2)   194

  11. Practicing Radical Vulnerability (Step 3)   209

  12. Obeying What God Tells You to Do (Step 4)   221

      Epilogue: "Go in the Strength You Have"   233

      Acknowledgments   237

      More Resources   241

      Notes   243

Preface

I really had no idea why I was there. I sat in the farthest chair at the farthest table in the back of the room.

I had been invited to a gathering for leaders of Christian men's and dads' ministries. While I didn't meet that criteria, a friend had helped organize the group, and I wanted to support him. So I showed up.

About thirty seconds into the first panel discussion, the epiphany happened.

"We need to stop focusing so much on dads who create companies, become multimillionaires, and then build a bunch of orphanages in Africa," one passionate panelist with a thick Southern drawl said. "I'm thankful for those people, but I just don't think a lot of us can relate to those guys. And we need stories we can relate to, not stories that make us feel less than."

Even though I was raised in a charismatic denomination, I had long ago left my vocal "amens" behind. But I couldn't help but let one slip out. If I'd had one of my mom's many shofars, I probably would have blown it.

That's because those words confirmed a major reason why I needed to write this book: to offer you a story you can truly relate to.

What story is that? I'm a Christian who, despite my faith, *became* an alcoholic. Despite knowing what I shouldn't do, I did it. Despite knowing what I should do, I *didn't* do it. For so many reasons that we'll cover. And it nearly destroyed me. Yet, even at my lowest point, many of those closest to me had no idea.

So that's why I'm here. To offer you not an example of dramatic salvation but of messy sanctification. In the end, I think the Church (big C, meaning the global body of all believers) likes to focus on stories of dramatic conversion, but it's not a big fan of stories of sanctification—especially messy sanctification. I'll explain all that more in a bit, but sanctification is the lifelong process that happens *after* we meet Jesus. Salvation is a lifeline; sanctification is a lifetime.

Don't get me wrong; it's powerful to listen to stories of the rock star who finds Jesus and throws his life and drugs on the altar. I'm a big fan of those stories. But I think we need more stories that mirror everyday life.

So I'm telling *my* story instead. A story of someone who has known Jesus since a very young age, followed him, loved him, and even helped others embrace him—and yet I fell hard into addiction. Someone who was drowning not outside the church but inside of it. Someone who could say all the right things with one breath and then gasp for air with the next.

Maybe you have a similar story. You know Jesus, you follow him, but in your imperfect way of doing so, you've found yourself gripped by something—a secret (or not so secret) sin, so to speak. Maybe what's gripping you is alcoholism, like it was me. Maybe it's porn. Maybe it's narcissism. Maybe it's drugs or adultery or bulimia. Whatever it is, my point in writing this book is to let you know that you're not alone, that there is hope for you. In fact, I think there are way more people like you and me in the church today than we realize—people who are stuck in secrets, sin, shame, and addiction.

Maybe you realize that already. Maybe you don't. Maybe you're desperate. Maybe you're just starting to suspect something. Maybe you're curious. I want you to know you have a seat right next to me. Maybe that's at the campfire, the dining room table, or the diner booth. Whatever makes you feel most comfortable. It's you and me, and I'm going to go first.

Roughly, that will look like this:

- I'll start by properly defining *alcoholism*. It's not as obvious as you think. In fact, because I got the definition wrong, I stayed stuck longer than I should have.
- Then I'm going to tell you my story because we gravitate toward stories. It's the most ancient form of communication.
- I'll then unpack how and why I got to the point I did, talking about things like shame and trauma.
- And finally, I'm going to walk you through the steps I took to break free.

Along the way, we're going to meet some people who have helped me in my recovery. Some of them you may already know—teachers like Matt Chandler, John Piper, Tim Keller, Brennan Manning, and John Mark Comer, as well as shame researchers Brené Brown and Curt Thompson. Others you may not, like self-described "Christian drunk" Heather Kopp, identity expert Jamie Winship, and counselors David Powlison, Alison Cook, Chuck DeGroat, and Debra Fileta. Each one has helped me make sense of addiction, recovery, myself, and Jesus—especially in my first year of sobriety. And I think it's important to convene subject-matter experts because I don't pretend to have all the answers. This book is a resource pointing you inward, outward, and upward.

Let me be clear about something, though: I'm not here to condemn you. No, our mistakes describe us; they don't define us. Instead, I'm here to help you. Not out of superiority but out of genuine care. Friend, I get you. Some days I wish I didn't because that process was painful. But I've resolved this: I'm not going to waste that pain. In reality, God's not going to waste it.

So right here, right now, you and I are going to go on a journey together. I'm going to be radically vulnerable with you, intimately detailed for you, and brutally honest about you. That's what God has called me to do in order to help you.

But I have one request as we begin: I need you to be honest, vulnerable, and detailed with yourself and with God. As ideas, convictions, or even disagreements pop up, write them down. Voice memo them. Fill these margins with notes—whatever you normally do to capture your thoughts, especially the thoughts you've been too scared to admit out loud.

Why? Because chances are, you're looking for things to be different. And I've learned that when you note the things changing inside you, more often than not things start changing around you.

So take note. Take heart. And take a seat. It's time we talked for a bit.

— Jon

Introduction

Blitzed on the Beach

"Just promise me you won't get drunk," my wife, Brett, said as I walked out of our hotel room in Miami.

We were on our fourteen-year anniversary trip. Every year we try to pick somewhere new to visit, and that year it was South Beach. This getaway was supposed to be particularly special: We were both craving respite after a very stressful season. We needed this trip, but Brett especially did.

That makes what I'm about to detail even tougher.

"Don't worry," I said, somewhat dismissively. "I promise." In reality, she had every reason to be worried. I knew it. She knew it.

It was Saturday night of the long Memorial Day weekend. After spending the past two days on the beach and using the evenings to walk up and down Ocean Drive, Brett wanted a quiet night in. I wasn't opposed. I'm a huge sports fan, and it just so happened that the NBA's Boston Celtics were playing the Miami Heat in a crucial playoff matchup.

I knew exactly what I wanted to do.

I saw the night in as a prime opportunity to "relax" at the hotel bar and grab a few drinks and appetizers while I watched the game. But Brett knew my history. "A few drinks" has always been hard for me. Once I start, I just keep going.

What's the point if you're not getting buzzed?

Over the years, I had tried different methods to curb my drinking and my propensity to get buzzed as fast as possible. At times, that looked like limiting myself to two drinks or even completely giving up alcohol for weeks or months at a time.

Even when successful, it never lasted.

Given the circumstances, "two drinks" wasn't my plan that night. I was on vacation. The big game was on TV in the very town where the matchup was being played. The environment was electric. I was going to give myself a bigger leash.

And as the saying goes, sometimes when you're given enough rope, you hang yourself.

I can honestly say that rarely in my life have I set out to get drunk. Plastered. Whatever word you want to use. I've never said to myself, "I'm drinking until I can't stand, can't remember anything, or can't help but throw up. I'm having *fun* tonight!" That night in Miami was the same. While I planned on having more than just two drinks, I didn't plan on getting drunk.

But like so many times before, it played out exactly the way you can imagine for a guy writing a book on alcohol. Two drinks led to three. Three led to five. And then the number gets a little fuzzy after that. The drink du jour was a house special: a gin martini with an onion garnish. I love gin. I love onions. The bartender warned me they were strong, though.

All the better, I thought.

Introduction

The basketball game didn't help. It was an intense back-and-forth contest, and I'm a fidgeter. As I'm writing this, I have a large insulated mug next to me. After every few sentences, I take a sip of the flavored water inside. I do that throughout the day to keep my hands occupied. When the drink next to me is of the alcoholic variety, then it's a bad combination.

Needless to say, I kept the bartender busy.

Over the years, I developed a lot of excuses to drink.

I'm happy. Drink.

I'm sad. Drink.

I'm excited. Drink.

I'm mad. Drink.

I'm cooking. Drink.

I'm sitting. Drink.

I'm doing yard work. Drink.

I'm relaxing. Drink.

I'm anxious. Drink.

I'm calm. Drink.

I'm watching TV. Drink.

I'm reading. Drink.

I'm having a bad day. Drink.

I'm having a good day. Drink.

I'm in a good place. Drink.

I'm ashamed. Drink a lot.

Nearly every opportunity and circumstance fit into some bucket of "Well, this calls for a drink." And when the home team lost in heartbreaking fashion? That definitely fit the bill. I was drinking in solidarity with the town, after all. So I drank some more. After my last round, though, it hit me: *Jon, you're drunk. Like, really drunk.*

I had broken my promise. Again. I was gone, my fine motor skills were shot, and the lobby was spinning. By this time, it was late in the evening, probably close to midnight. I knew that in my current state I couldn't return to the hotel room. Even though Brett was likely sleeping, the shame immediately took over. Like Adam and Eve in the garden, I wanted to hide. To run. So that's what I did.

After paying the bar tab, which was well north of $100, I shuffled through the front doors of the hotel and onto South Beach. I knew I had to try and sober up, and the only thing that could do that was time. I zigzagged my way down to the ocean, sat down in the sand, and started beating myself up.

Who are you, Jon? Why can't you stop? Why does this have so much control over you? Why can't you drink like a normal person? What is Brett going to say? You're an idiot! Maybe you should just end it all; that's the only way you'll break free.

As I swore at myself and the shame crashed over me like the waves I was staring at, I realized I had to pee. Anyone even remotely close to me will tell you this: I have a bladder the size of an almond. I can have one Coke Zero, and within minutes of finishing it, I'm headed to the bathroom. So after countless drinks, you can imagine how badly I needed to use the bathroom.

But what do you do when you're sitting on the beach in the pitch-black with no bathroom in sight? Especially when there are people around. I had only one option in my mind.

I stood up shakily and headed for the water. With all my clothes on, I stumbled into the ocean. And I kept walking until the water reached my neck. There, I relieved myself. It came out of both ends. And as I looked back to the shore, I saw what my life had become. I saw what alcohol had done to me. I saw a metaphor

Introduction

for where I was headed if I kept down this road—drunk, alone, standing in my own waste, and maybe even drowning. My salty tears hit the salty water, and I sobbed.

But I didn't know what to do. How to stop it. How to change course. I was lost. I was ashamed. I was broken. The next day would give me answers, but they would be painful.

― ― ―

I woke up late the next morning with a massive hangover. I remember Brett nudging me earlier and saying she was going to get some breakfast but I could sleep in. After a little more time in bed, I came to and started recalling the night before.

More shame. More questions. More self-flogging.

To be clear, I remember everything from that night. I wasn't blackout drunk. In fact, I'm not sure I've ever been truly blackout drunk, where I don't remember *anything*. I'm missing bits and pieces here and there but never whole evenings.* But if you have a drinking problem, you'll recognize what I'm about to say: I used that "I'm not getting blackout drunk" as an excuse to tell myself that I didn't really have an issue.

Alcoholics get blackout drunk, I'd tell myself. *And since I'm not getting blackout drunk, I'm fine.*†

I wasn't. And I was finally starting to realize that.

In fact, just a few weeks earlier, I had used the term *alcoholic* to describe myself for the first time. Brett and I were invited to a couples' retreat in Georgia by a mentor. We thought it was going to be a relaxing few days of nothingness. We were wrong.

---

* What I was experiencing is called a "brownout" or a "grayout." And brownouts and grayouts are still bad.

† We'll cover the term *alcoholic* in chapter 2 and properly define it. We'll also cover the comparison game so many of us play with ourselves.

21

Instead, the focus (which we only truly realized once we arrived) was on abiding with Christ, listening for and to his voice, and acting in obedience. But the first evening, I noticed the host had one of the best bourbon collections I'd ever seen, and I've never met a bourbon I couldn't like. Over the years, I've traveled to middle-of-nowhere liquor stores to find rare ones. Local liquor stores had gotten to know me by name and even had me on secret lists to call when they got something "good." I was well acquainted with the back rooms and store managers. As such, I've spent thousands of dollars on bourbon in my lifetime.

So when the retreat host broke out the nice cigars and fine bourbon, I was elated. The men went outside to drink, smoke, and talk, while the women cracked open bottles of wine and champagne inside. Halfway through the late evening, Brett's head peeked around the corner.

"I'm headed to bed," she said before looking at me seriously and mouthing, "Promise me you won't get drunk." It was a common phrase from her to me.

"I'm good," I said, again dismissively. "I promise."

I did, in fact, get drunk. I regularly snuck away to the bathroom due to my bladder, only to refill my bourbon glass again and again and again when no one was looking.

I can say I got *drunk* now, by the way, with a lot of clarity. In the past, I would say I just got *buzzed*. But in my heart, I know the difference. The night ended with me fumbling back to my bed in the bunkhouse located a few hundred yards away from the main house. On the way, I saw a bottle of expensive champagne that was bound for the trash but still had a little left in it. I grabbed it and nursed it on the way back.

The next day, the intense work of learning how to abide in Christ began. Every word cut straight to my soul. Every exercise made me sick inside. The Holy Spirit wasn't stirring inside me; he was cutting swaths through the jungle of my soul. He was sanding down the calluses I had built up, specifically around my relationship with alcohol.

That afternoon, we were dismissed individually with instructions to spend time with God and listen to what he was telling us. I already knew what he was telling me. He was screaming it. I walked outside to a white picket fence and began bawling as two horses stared me down. Tears streamed down my face. After a while, another man on the retreat joined me. He was crying over what God was telling him as well. As he put his hand on my back, the words tumbled out.

"I think I'm an alcoholic," I said through heaves.

It felt good to say it. There was a weight that was lifted—not completely off, but at least I could breathe. After calming down, I found Brett and told her my conclusion. You might think this is the place where she enthusiastically agrees, cries, we hug, and the road to recovery begins.

Not at all.

Brett was actually a little cautious. "I don't know if you're an alcoholic, but you definitely have turned to alcohol as your main coping mechanism," she said. I was a little confused. Wasn't it obvious?

What I would come to understand later is that, while Brett was worried about my drinking, she was more worried about *why* I was drinking. The root, not just the fruit. She didn't want me to hide—yes, hide—behind the term *alcoholic*. In other words, she didn't want me to be able to use the term to justify not doing a deeper dive. What she wanted was for me to get to the bottom of it *all*.

But in my mind, I thought that maybe, just *maybe*, she didn't know the extent to which I had started covering up how much I was drinking. How I would hide the beer cans and bottles, how I would try and drink as much as I could before she came home from work or an outing so the "buzz" would carry me through the evening, or how I'd fib about how much I had to drink when she asked me.

She did know a lot of it. Maybe not all, but a lot. We alcoholics think we are so clever, don't we? And while I thought I was a master magician, she carried that knowledge like a weight around her heart that I've only recently come to realize.

That's also because there was something else at play: In the past, when Brett would bring up my drinking, I didn't respond well. I'd get defensive. Angry. Dismissive. I'd turn it around on her. *Gaslighting* is the term now. And that's what I would do. I would gaslight her. Not surprisingly, then, she had learned how to tread lightly around the topic, even if *I* brought it up. On top of that, some close friends of ours had witnessed some of the drunken aftermath when I got back to the bunkhouse and she was humiliated. So instead of making it a "bigger thing" right then and there, she chose the high road. Just one more example of how incredibly wise—but also incredibly hurt—she was.

So with all that at play, we agreed to unpack both what I said and what she said at a later date and keep it an ongoing conversation over the next few weeks. But not surprisingly, I used her comments as a justification. As a green light.

See, Jon, it's not even as bad as you think it is! Even Brett agrees. That's not what she was saying at all, but that's what I wanted to hear. That's what the disease aspect wanted to hear. And there is a disease aspect.*

So after taking a break from alcohol for a couple weeks, I used the Miami anniversary trip as a treat for being so good with my recent

---

* I'll talk about this more, but the disease is both physical *and* spiritual. That's an important distinction. There are those who disagree it's spiritual and those who disagree it's physical. I don't think it's an either/or but a both/and.

drinking. I roll my eyes at myself just thinking about that. But if you want to know how I went from calling myself an alcoholic a few weeks earlier to being drunk alone on South Beach, that's how it happened. I think that's the story of so many of us who realize we have an issue. There isn't always this clean, pretty line from realizing we have a problem to actually addressing it fully.

As I stirred in the hotel room, I cursed the light trying to peek through the curtains as my wife enjoyed a beachside breakfast. Alone. The image from the night before returned.

Look what your drinking has done.

When I finally regained enough of my equilibrium to get dressed and head downstairs, I checked my phone and saw a text from Brett telling me that she had already made her way to the beach. I must have fallen back asleep earlier while beating myself up. Self-deprecation can be tiring. I changed into my trunks and headed down to meet her.

As I sauntered up to her lounge chair under an umbrella in the sand, we started making small talk. Pretty quickly, the question I had been dreading came out of her mouth.

"Did you get drunk last night?" she asked with a slight smirk. (The smirk, once again, was the result of her training herself to tread lightly.)

"Nope," I said. "Maybe a little buzzed, but the game was pretty intense and came down to the last shot." I shocked myself with how quickly the lie poured out. No hesitation. No visible qualms. It was effortless. And it scared me.

"OK," she said and went back to reading her book.

Two more times shortly after that, she asked again. "You *promise* you weren't drunk last night?"

"No, I promise." But like a good lawyer, she was asking a question she already knew the answer to. And like Peter, I denied it three times.

If I was torn up after the first lie, I was absolutely a wreck inside as the day went on. Throughout the trip, we didn't drink on the beach. We didn't even eat lunch. We saved all that for the evening. Around 3:00 p.m., we'd start scrolling Yelp and looking for a good restaurant where we could have an early dinner before the crowds and, ironically, the drunk tourists got bad. That day, we found a highly rated Latin joint and made reservations.

As we headed to the room, changed, and set out for the restaurant, my insides felt like they were in a vise. My chest was tight. My mouth was dry. I couldn't believe that I had lied to Brett not once, not twice, but three times about what happened the night before, especially after feeling like I had hit rock bottom in the ocean and especially after coming to the conclusion I had weeks earlier about my relationship with alcohol.

I knew what I had to do. The Holy Spirit was making my next move clear: I had to tell Brett not only what had happened the night before but that I had lied about it. I knew what it would do to her, though. It would wreck her. Still, it had to be done.

When we sat down at the restaurant, the waiter asked what we wanted to drink. Brett ordered some sort of sangria. Me? Only a Coke Zero.

We ordered our food, and when it finally came, I did little more than pick at it. I literally couldn't stomach it. After a few minutes, I put down my fork, looked up at Brett, and started in.

"Hey, I have to tell you something," I said. My voice got shaky, and my eyes started to water. "Earlier when you asked me if I had gotten drunk, I lied to you. I did get drunk last night, and I'm really sorry about that." There was a part of me that hoped that would be enough, but the other part knew it wouldn't.

She looked at me with deep hurt. Almost immediately, she got up and excused herself. She went to the bathroom for what seemed like a couple hours. I was left to sit there in my sin. Sit there and just let it crawl over every fiber of my being like some flesh-eating amoeba. I was sure everyone in the restaurant could see the life leaving my body.

When she finally returned, eyes red and the most defeated look I had ever seen on her face, she broke her silence.

"You want to know what hurts the most?" she asked with increased exasperation and her voice cracking. "I *knew* you were lying to me. I just *knew* it. That's why I asked you three times. But I chose to let it go.

"Why?" she continued. "Why did you lie? I'm not even that upset about the drinking part, but why did you lie? Do you know what that does to me as a woman and a wife? If it's so easy for you to lie about this, what else have you and *will* you lie about?"

I didn't have much to say. In all honesty, I froze. We have a fight, flight, or freeze mechanism. I tend to freeze during conflict. I'm like a deer in the proverbial headlights. I knew I had to muster something, though. So I said the only thing I could.

"I'm sorry. I truly am. I don't know why I lied. I was embarrassed. I'm sorry. I need help."

She didn't respond. That was my cue. I asked for the check, paid, and we started down the street in complete silence.

As we worked our way through the growingly crowded Miami sidewalks, we were "together," but there was a chasm between us. We didn't have a destination in mind—at least not a spoken one—so we just walked. And walked. And walked some more. Before long, we found ourselves on the beach, nearly at the same exact spot where I had seen my drunken future sprawled out before me the night before.

As we sat down, neither of us could muster any words. I began digging a hole in the sand. If I could get it big enough, maybe I could crawl into it. It was Brett who finally broke the silence.

"Jon, I'm really not upset about the drinking. Honestly," she said. Her tone was soft. But it was dejected. It wasn't filled with anger or shame. It was genuine hurt. I would have handled anger better, honestly. This cut me more than a profanity-laced tirade, which I absolutely deserved.

"I'm upset that you lied to me—*three times*," she emphasized as she continued. "But what I'm really torn up about is that we continue to find ourselves here."

"I know," I interrupted. But she stopped me.

"Let me finish," she said. Husbands, when your wife says "let me finish," you'd best be quiet. So I shut up.

"Throughout our entire marriage, you've *never* dealt with your underlying issues. You have trauma in your past, and you just jump from thing to thing to try and deal with it. That's why it's not about the drinking for me. Because even if you never take another drink, it's just going to be something else that you turn to until you address what's going on beneath the surface."

Now I really wanted to crawl into the hole I was digging. She was right. My childhood was filled with trauma. There was sexual trauma. There was my dad leaving us. There was my sister's behavioral and drug issues that created more chaos—both physical and emotional—than I could even begin to explain. There were other forms of abuse. And there was my diagnosed anxiety and OCD.

The last one—the anxiety and OCD—had been better for a while. I had made a lot of strides over the years, even culminating in a bestselling Christian book on the topic in 2021.

But the other things? I had never dealt with them. I had pushed them down. In fact, there are aspects of them I refused to even acknowledge. So when a series of difficult circumstances over the previous two years cracked the crust of my resolve and my spirit, I began spewing all sorts of hot, destructive lava on myself and those around me. That meant my anxiety had returned and was at an all-time high. I was in the throes of a deep depression. Overwhelmed, confused, and whatever other term you want to throw in there, I turned to an easy fix, an easy coping mechanism.

I turned to alcohol.

In the past, I had turned to porn. I had turned to work. I had turned to codependent relationships. I had turned to food. I had even turned to alcohol for periods. But this was worse. And that meant my at-times unhealthy relationship with alcohol had turned into a full-blown drinking problem.

"Yeah, you're right," I said through more tears. I'm pretty sure we raised the ocean level that evening with how much we cried.

"Here's what I'm asking: It's not to stop drinking; it's to get into intensive therapy and get to the root of *why* you're drinking this way. That's what I want. That's how you can show me you're really sorry," she said. "Email the therapist we've been talking about."

"The therapist" was a local counselor we had heard about who specialized in a form of trauma therapy called eye movement desensitization and reprocessing (EMDR) therapy. So without hesitation, I took out my phone and pulled up the woman's website. I clicked on the contact button, and I typed out this message:

> Hey Gina,
>
> I got your name from a friend. I've been interested in starting EMDR therapy. I have diagnosed anxiety and OCD. And while it's generally been under control, it has gotten really bad lately and is manifesting itself in some harmful ways. I also believe there is trauma in my past

that I have yet to fully deal with. Would love to start soon if you have an opening.

Jon

I hit send at 7:31 p.m., turned my phone toward Brett so the glow lit up her now-puffy eyes, and showed it to her.

"Thank you," she said softly. She grabbed my hand and put her head on my shoulder. As Memorial Day fireworks exploded over the ocean, I buried my nose in her hair and let the tears wet her scalp. She didn't care.

I was scared, but I was hopeful. I was exhausted, but anticipatory. I was broken, but I felt healing was possible. For the first time ever, I thought I could maybe break free from the grip drinking had on my life.

We left Miami a day later. The idea of making a commitment right then and there to never have another drop of alcohol was too much for me. It scared me. In a weird way, it made me sad. So I didn't do it. Instead, every morning, I committed to not drinking that day. And I renewed that commitment daily.

The therapist, Gina, did get back to me. However, she couldn't see me until mid-June. Until then, I had to wait and do things on my own. It's not like I didn't have any tools available to me. In fact, I had written in the past about some of the tools in my toolbox; I had just abandoned them. So I started implementing those. I upped my running regimen. I began the process of "abiding" with Christ every morning, like we had been taught at the retreat a few weeks earlier. I asked Brett to hide all of my bourbon.

And you know what started happening? I was miserable. Yes, I was miserable.

Introduction

One thing you're going to see throughout this book is that I'm radically honest and radically vulnerable. I'm not going to lie to you and say that everything instantly got better—that the sun started shining brighter, the birds began singing just to me, and my life got so much easier.

No, in fact, it got worse.

Quitting drinking cold turkey revealed how much of a problem it had become. At the time I quit, I was drinking every night. I was getting "buzzed" every night. The number of drinks it took me to get to that point had steadily grown, though. It was probably three to four bourbons or five to six high-ABV (alcohol by volume) beers. And by the end, I was sliding into drunkenness more often than not.

That means when I stopped, I went through withdrawal. I didn't get the shakes, but I did have night sweats. For at least a week after the Miami trip, I woke up in the middle of every night drenched. Sometimes I would even have to change pajamas.

That scared me.*

The other thing that happened? I wandered aimlessly. No, really. Drinking had become my main activity. Not my wife, not my kids—my drinking. And with my nightly routine of several drinks gone, the main coping mechanism I had to deal with the circumstances that led to my recurrence of severe anxiety and depression was gone too.

So in the evenings, when my mind would race the most and I loathed being with my own thoughts, I didn't know what to do with myself. So, what *did* I do? I would literally pace my home. Sometimes it was the living room, other times it was my office,

---

* If your drinking sounds like mine, I encourage you to seek professional help if you've decided to stop. I've learned over the years that quitting cold turkey when you've been drinking as much as I was could actually kill you. And I want you around.

other times it was my garage. I couldn't stay still. I didn't want to stay still. I had forgotten what it was like to deal with my thoughts and be with myself in a healthy way. I was restlessly bored.*

So I paced. And at times I cried out, "God! You have to help me!"

Sometimes he answered me by giving me peace, sometimes by making me tired. But many times, he let me sit in that feeling like a high school athlete who had just lost a state championship. I am so grateful, by the way, for that. Why? Because I had to learn how to sit with myself again. I had to learn healthy coping mechanisms. I had to learn to turn to him, even for the littlest things, like getting to sleep (whereas, before, alcohol took care of that).

That process is messy. It's not fun. And it's hard.

My first session with Gina was June 21. From the moment I walked into her office, I knew she was special. She is the kindest, most soft-spoken and motherly woman I have ever met. I think she could moonlight as a voice actress for a sleep app.

I immediately felt safe. That was important because I needed to tell her everything. And I mean everything. Sure, about the drinking. But I needed to tell her about my shame. The past sexual trauma. All the insecurities. The thoughts that I just couldn't shake. The other coping mechanisms I had turned to in the past. The lies I believed about myself and about God.

And for the first few sessions, that's exactly what we did. I talked, she listened. Before we could get to the specialized EMDR therapy, she needed me to walk her through my life up to that point. Not surprisingly, that took several sessions. Once again, it wasn't easy.

---

* It didn't help that a recent car accident had affected Brett's health, and many nights she would need to retire to bed early, leaving me alone.

I began dredging up feelings that I had either suppressed or never felt before.

Enter my relapse.

After two sessions with Gina, we hit the Fourth of July holiday weekend. While I felt safe during and after our sessions, that didn't mean I felt good. I was hopeful, but that was interrupted by moments of helplessness. While Gina and I had started down a road of recovery and healing, I was still in the ER era of my therapy.

So when we ended up at my in-laws' lake house for the holiday, I wasn't ready for the flood of triggers and emotions that were waiting for me. As many of you can probably attest to, long weekends and holidays are excuses to drink—a lot. They mean you can start earlier than normal, they mean you can drink longer than normal, and they mean you don't have to face the consequences like normal. That's how I had come to treat holidays, especially over the previous two years.

I entered the weekend committed to not drinking. I left the weekend having caved in on the last night, sneaking a handful of hard seltzers I found in the back of the fridge.

That small compromise—and hiding it from Brett—meant that later in the week, when we returned to reality and stress, I fully gave in. That Friday, after a long week, I went to the liquor store while Brett was at work and bought a large bottle of my favorite "everyday drinker"—a bourbon that's neither expensive nor disgustingly cheap. At 3:00 p.m., I tore into it like a kid on Christmas. Glass after glass after glass. By the time Brett got home from work, I was already buzzed. By the time she and the kids went to bed, I was drunk.

For a little bit, it felt good. But quickly, the shame washed over me. And that's when the thoughts of suicide took over.

Brett and the kids deserve someone better than this, I told myself. *You're the "Christian mental health" guy, and look at you. If your readers, if your publisher, if all those people that interviewed you could see you now, they would cancel you in an instant. You're a fake and a fraud. Just get it over with already. At least it will save Brett and the kids some embarrassment and be on your terms. Brett truly deserves a better husband, and the kids truly deserve a better father.*

I'd struggled with suicidal thoughts in the past, but hadn't had intense ones like this in some time. Even the ones that plagued me on the beach in Miami weren't this bad. I think that's because I had already made some progress, only to find myself right back to square one.

By God's grace, I didn't act on any of those thoughts. Instead, I crawled to bed and waited for the sun to rise.

It did. It always does.

When I told Brett, she was disappointed but surprisingly very gracious. She pointed out how I had dredged up a lot from my past in just my first two sessions with Gina, and it wasn't shocking that I had turned to my go-to coping mechanism as a result. She didn't shame me; she supported me.

I felt better, but I didn't feel good. While what Brett said explained my actions, it didn't excuse them. I emailed Gina immediately after and told her what happened, ahead of our regularly scheduled appointment two days from then. I once again committed to not drinking for that day. And then the day after. I began reading voraciously. An elder at my church had once recommended the Alcoholics Anonymous "Big Book" after I had confided in him years earlier that I was drinking more than I wanted to (although I wasn't completely honest about *everything*). I finally opened it up. I learned a lot about myself, and many of the stories resonated with me. I also doubled down on my commitment to abide with

Christ, read my Bible every morning, and spend intentional time with God, even if only for a few minutes to begin with. And that, in chorus with my ongoing therapy with Gina, began producing a change within me.

Like a desert flower tasting rain for the first time, I began to open up. The prickly, ugly parts of me started giving way to something cautiously beautiful. My shame, for example, began turning into genuine remorse. I began to grieve what I had been doing to myself, my family, and God. I began to see how my actions were grieving *others*.

From there, new flowers started blooming. I started seeing that I wasn't the sum of my mistakes. As I opened up my Bible more, I started seeing that my story—the starts, the stops, the one step forward, two steps back—was littered throughout the Word of God. I saw that you can love Jesus and still struggle with sins, even embarrassing ones. I began believing that I was able to be fully loved by God. I began focusing on letting him invade every crack of my soul, and as I did that, a new hope flooded over me.

Throughout the next year of my life, that hope only grew. Soft rains started forming a stream in the desert. The aha moments came regularly. And as I continued to pursue Jesus more and more, I discovered the stream led to an oasis that looked like a process to break free from destructive drinking—a process that can be used to break free from a lot of unhealthy habits in our lives.

A process that has kept me sober and led to a true, genuine, and lasting transformation.

This book is about that transformation process, which includes four key steps: abiding in Christ, finding your true identity, practicing radical vulnerability, and obeying what God tells you to do. I don't pretend it's the only way to break free, but I know it is

Introduction

definitely a *way* to break free (and to stay free). And I also know it's not going to hurt you. It can't, because it's rooted in Scripture.

But this book isn't *only* about that process.

It's also about how I got to the point that I got to—the lowest point in my life. It's about how the journey to destructive drinking—and to many other destructive habits—is often a slow fade. It's about properly defining the word *alcoholic* so that people like me don't have an excuse to continue down a path that leads to hurt and destruction. It's about how much more time I got back when I gave up drinking, how much more present I became, and how much more literal brain power I gained. It's about combating shame. It's about showing you that you're not alone. It's about giving you a better way to deal with your hurts, your traumas, and your pain. It's about how any relationship that is misordered is disordered and why our struggles with alcohol are both physical and spiritual.

But most importantly, it's about sanctification.

That word *sanctification* is a churchy word. You've probably heard it at some point. But what does it mean, really? I like the *New Oxford American Dictionary*'s definition: "The action or process of being freed from sin or purified."[1]

Did you pick up on the most important word there? It's a *process*. In other words, sanctification is continually becoming more like Jesus. It's learning. It's growing. It's even failing. And it assumes that where you were yesterday is not where you should be

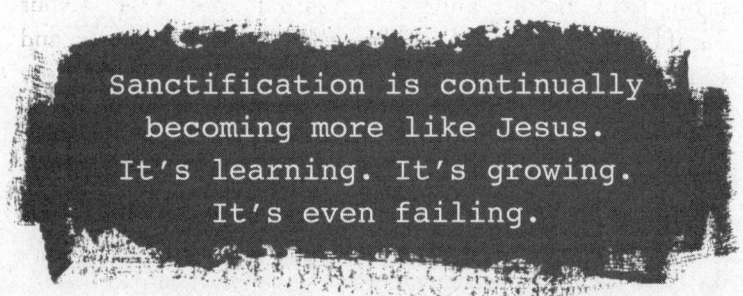

Introduction

tomorrow. It assumes that who you were when you decided to follow Jesus is not who you will be when you join him in heaven.

You know what that means? Sanctification—a key doctrine of the Christian faith—leaves room for messy stories. It leaves room for growth. It leaves room for writing a bestselling Christian book on mental health and a year and a half later hitting rock bottom while crapping your pants in the ocean—and then writing about *that* experience.

It means that whatever messy story you have is OK. It's OK.* You are not too far gone. Your struggle with alcohol—or whatever else—doesn't make you too dirty, too much of a hypocrite, too much of a fake for Jesus. Truth be told, the fact that you're reading these words right now means you're going through a sanctification process. You know who doesn't read a book like this? People who aren't being sanctified. The fact that there's even an inkling of interest shows that the Holy Spirit is at work inside of you.

That doesn't mean there aren't consequences for what you do. There are. There were for me. That doesn't mean you won't face questions. That doesn't mean this journey won't be hard. That doesn't mean you won't be discouraged. And I'm going to be *really* honest with you: That doesn't mean others—even other Christians—will completely understand, support, or accept your messy story.

But that's exactly what sanctification is for—the messy stories. Sanctification doesn't, and can't, just look like cursing like a sailor before Jesus and then only saying "darn it" for the rest of your life after praying "the sinner's prayer." Sanctification doesn't, and can't, *only* look like telling fewer little white lies, giving more money to the poor, or becoming a kinder person.

No, Jesus welcomes big, messy stories. God placed them throughout the Bible for a reason. And while it's costly to welcome those

---

* As I once heard Pastor Matt Chandler say, though, "It's OK to not be OK. But it's not OK to stay that way." That's a wise caveat.

stories and the people behind them, that's what the church is called to do.

Fitting, because I believe there are far more of the messy stories out there than anyone realizes. There are far more Christians getting drunk on South Beach than we imagine. There are far more people who know and love Jesus but are still battling very specific—very big—issues that are holding them back from a joyful, peaceful, purposeful, and abundant life with Christ. There are far more strugglers than there are "saints."

There are far more people like me, and probably like you.

If that's true, read on. Read on for hope, for help, for him—the "him" who both loves you and is weaving together all the aspects of your beautiful, messy story.

PART 1

MY STORY

ONE

Drunk at Deer Camp

The truth is I've only ever had one addiction. The white whale of addictions: escape.
—Lara Love Hardin, *The Many Lives of Mama Love*

I still vividly remember the first time I got drunk. I was around fourteen.

In Wisconsin, where I'm from, there are three things that get you through the long, brutally cold winters: Green Bay Packers football, deer hunting season, and drinking. My baptism by firewater came at the hands of the last two.

I had a mentor growing up who was part father, part grandfather. He was old enough to be the latter, but he treated me like he was the former. His name was Chuck. He had a slightly bulbous nose, slack jowls, a large bald spot with a few stubborn hairs still holding on, and a gut that was neither massive nor minimal. While he and his wife were family friends, Chuck went out of his way to seek me out and invest in me, for reasons I'll never fully understand.

There are so many good parts of who I am today that he took out of himself and placed in me.

Chuck was an engineer, a deep thinker, a tinkerer who listened to classical music in the garage, and especially an avid outdoorsman. He was both a skilled fisherman and a hunter, of everything from deer to ducks.

Over the course of my preteen and teenage years, he introduced me to Tchaikovsky, taught me how to blow a goose call in between chess lessons, showed me how to load a primitive black-powder rifle, explained the difference between AC and DC electrical currents, and gave me weekly lessons on American and Wisconsin history. He would always proudly remind me that his French ancestors helped settle our area of the Badger State. With my hectic home life, I would spend weeks with him and his wife over the summers.

When he died, I felt like I had lost a family member. And at the funeral, his wife embraced me like I was one.

One particular early December day, I found myself with Chuck a few hours from our hometown, hunting deer with one of his old friends, Hank. All my previous deer hunting attempts were unsuccessful, so Chuck sat me in the best spot: on the ground, among some barren trees overlooking a plowed, snow-frosted field. And I waited.

After no activity, he quietly maneuvered around the back of the adjoining woods and started walking in my direction in hopes of funneling a deer toward me.

It worked.

The doe ("a deer, a female deer") stepped into the field cautiously. Because I was using one of the primitive rifles Chuck taught me to use (think something close to what they used during the Civil War), I needed the animal to get close. Soon enough, she came within about fifty yards. But fifty yards was still at the top of the rifle's range. If I was going to pull the trigger, it had to be the perfect shot.

In one quiet motion, I raised my rifle, cocked the hammer, and aimed near the top of her back, just behind the front shoulder, trying to account for the drop of the solid lead ball once it started traveling. I pulled the trigger, and after the white sulfur cloud dissipated, I saw her run back into the woods. I removed my stocking cap so I could listen. And that's when I heard the crash.

I had gotten my first deer.

After about ten minutes of waiting, I heard Chuck yell and confirm it. He had seen her fall, and he was as excited for me as I was for myself.

After dinner, we all gathered in Hank's living room to celebrate and recount the story. They kept complimenting my shot and that I'd had the wherewithal to aim high to compensate for the distance. I couldn't get enough of the praise.

But there was something else I couldn't get enough of.

See, on the way to Hank's house, we stopped at a liquor store and bought a *gallon* of cheap red table wine. Carlo Rossi. I can still see the white label with the old man on the front and the cursive signature used as the logo. Chuck and Hank had a tradition at deer camp of drinking the stuff. It was half joke and full ritual.

As we settled in, Chuck asked if I wanted a glass to celebrate my first deer and my good shot. I had drank before with family members, so it wasn't that odd. In Wisconsin, and many other states, having a drink with your parents or guardian is legal. For some, their parents allowing them to drink with them while underage demystifies alcohol altogether. And in Wisconsin, the practice is as normal as a ten-inch January snowfall.

I accepted.

When I took the first drink from the very full glass, I had nothing to compare it to. I had never drank wine before. I couldn't tell you if it was good or bad. But what I could tell you is that shortly after finishing it off, I felt something. Something different. Something lighter. Something good. My mouth moved faster while my brain moved slower. I was in the moment. The racing thoughts and beating heart I had grown so accustomed to as my "normal" abated. I would come to learn in my adulthood that I had been living with undiagnosed anxiety and OCD for most of my life. And this liquid, this serum, made me feel better. It took the troubles away.

We laughed and became animated as we talked about everything from the hunt to politics to sports. And I wanted more of it. More of the moment, more of the feeling, and more of the wine.

I had to have more of the wine.

I remember refilling my glass several times throughout the evening. Sometimes I would say I needed to go to the bathroom, which I did, but I was always sure to top myself off. Sometimes Chuck and Hank would ask me to refill their glasses as well, and I would make sure I didn't leave my own half empty. When it comes to drinking, I've learned that I'm a glass fully full kind of guy.

Near the end of the evening, which may have been morning, I remember telling Hank how much I loved Chuck and was thankful for all he had done for me. That was probably Chuck's cue; I think he cut me off shortly after that, but I couldn't tell you for sure.

And that's when the dream happened.

I dreamed I had gotten up and was stumbling through the house, looking for the bathroom. I dreamed that I had found the bathroom and was sitting on the floor. In the dream, I felt so bad, both physically and emotionally. Guilt. Shame. Sickness. I dreamed I was whimpering and moaning and throwing up.

Then I woke up.

When I finally rubbed the sleep out of my eyes, I realized I wasn't feeling well. I got out of bed and headed straight for the toilet. As I did, I noticed something: There were red splotches all over the white carpet of the house. And as I got closer to the bathroom, those red splotches turned into red streaks. And by the time I found the toilet, it looked like someone had been murdered on the floor with little attempt to cover it up.

That's when I realized: I didn't have a dream at all. No, the "dream" was me in a drunken stupor trying to find the bathroom. And in the process, I had absolutely destroyed the house as I spewed red wine and vomit, creating carpet stains that looked like crime-scene photos from a *Dateline* episode.

But I was still too hungover, or probably still too drunk, to do anything about it. I remember Chuck coming out of his own room after hearing me throw up again in the toilet, surveying the scene calmly, and telling me to change and go back to bed. I eventually woke up a second time to the sound of a carpet steamer Chuck had rented from the local Walmart.

No one said much as we packed up to leave. However, I did apologize to Hank, who was gracious. That was impressive, considering as we grabbed our things and walked out the door, I could still see faded pink stains dotting the floor like runway lights from the bedroom to the bathroom.

What have I done? I'm never drinking again.

I did drink underage again but never to the point of getting drunk.

While I know some people get that first taste of alcohol and that first buzz and descend quickly into a drinking problem, that wasn't me.

And yet, something was stirred in me that day. A seed was planted that would take decades to fully mature. But all the while, its roots were thickening. That seed was this: Drinking takes the edge off; drinking helps you escape; drinking brings relief.

I would return to deer camp throughout my adulthood, not physically but mentally. I would remember the feeling that drove me to keep refilling my wine glass. I would long for that relief. At deer camp, I learned that alcohol could help me forget my problems—the problems with my sister's growing behavioral issues, the problems with my stepdad's temper, the problems with my racing mind—if only for a few hours. And I never unlearned it.

I couldn't put the genie back in the wine bottle.

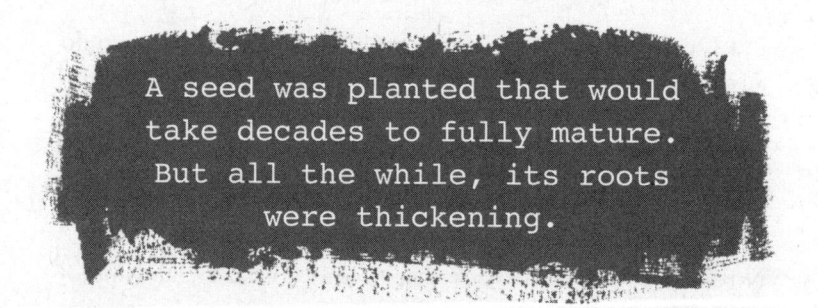

> A seed was planted that would take decades to fully mature. But all the while, its roots were thickening.

TWO

Am I an Alcoholic?

> I suppose we're all drunk on something.
> —Seth Haines, *Coming Clean*

During the summer of 2012, I distinctly remember how the hot Texas sun would beat down on the reddish concrete pool deck of our apartment complex. It's the first time I had experienced consistent triple-digit temperatures in my life. I grew up in Wisconsin, where we would declare a state of emergency if it hit ninety. Texas summers are a different animal. The local news literally shows people frying eggs on the pavement and cooking brisket in their cars every year.

That heat during my first summer in Texas did more than fry an egg and my skin, though; it gave me an excuse to drink.

Brett and I had recently moved from New York City to a yuppie-ish suburb just north of the Dallas city limits. We had been married for about three years at the time and were "DINKs"—dual income, no kids. That meant our weekends were wide open, and we had expendable income. If you have kids, especially younger kids, this statement will resonate with you: I will always wonder what we did with all that time, before baseball games and birthday parties and music lessons. We had so much of it.

However, if I'm honest, I don't have to wonder as much. Because during that summer, I started noticing an unhealthy pattern.

After going to church most Sunday mornings, we would get brunch or come home and snack on something before heading down with a cooler full of treats and beverages to beat the heat in the pool area. Early during that summer, the cooler's contents looked like sodas, water, and a few alcoholic beverages: beers for me, and something sweet for Brett. But as the summer burned on, the cooler's composition changed: more and more beers for me.

It's hot! And when it's hot, it's OK to drink more.

It wasn't long, though, before I started to feel like the afternoon was incomplete without a buzz. I was working in the news business at the time, which meant my weekdays were extremely stressful. I was in charge of a stable of writers, handing out assignments and managing the daily editorial operations of the website. I would start around 5:00 a.m. and, if I was lucky, log off around 2:00 p.m. But I was always on call, even on the weekends. I also had undiagnosed anxiety and OCD at the time. That made for a horrible combination. I couldn't turn my brain off, and I couldn't stop thinking about the stresses of work and the news cycle. I couldn't relax. So I began to treat my weekends as hall passes to "recharge," especially Sundays, since those were the slowest news days.

How did I do that? I took the easy way. I returned to deer camp. I again reacquainted myself with how effective having a little buzz was at allowing me to be more present during the time off—or at least less worried.* I used the alcohol as a levee to hold back the worries of the previous week and the onslaught of the upcoming one. And if some buzz was good, more was better.

---

* This wasn't the only time I'd do this. You'll read in the next chapter how it became a recurring theme.

How much more? I remember one Sunday stumbling up to our apartment and promptly throwing up in the toilet. When a surprised Brett (who had come up earlier) asked what happened, I told her that I had sucked down my beers too fast because of the heat, and someone at the pool had poured us shots of whipped cream–flavored vodka that just didn't sit well. That was partially true: The vodka *was* disgusting. But it didn't sit well because I kept drinking it. And drinking it. I wanted what it gave me, no matter what it tasted like. And while I preferred to get that buzz with something I enjoyed, I was willing to sacrifice taste for effects.

I returned to deer camp often that summer—to the relief of my racing mind. I wanted—I needed—that escape. But as the longer days started giving way to cooler temperatures, I started asking myself a very important question. In some ways, I only wanted to ask it in order to feel better about myself. I got to check the box for self-evaluation. Because, after all, only healthy people self-evaluate, right? So if I was asking the question, then I was healthy. I could stop there, take the win, and not have to face the answer—and especially the consequences.

It's a question I wouldn't answer honestly until over ten years later.

The Question

As I've told my story, I've learned the question I started asking myself that summer is an important question for a lot of strugglers. So important, in fact, I think we have to start our conversation with it, even before we get to the nitty-gritty of my story. Because we have to be on the same page about something crucial.

That question is this: **"Am I an alcoholic?"**

If you're reading this book, my guess is you've probably asked yourself that question. Maybe not as often as I have but probably at least once.

- Maybe you've committed to not drinking for a year, a month, a week, or a day and not been able to do it.
- Maybe you set out to "just have one or two" and ended up pretty buzzed. Maybe drunk. Maybe wasted. Maybe even blacked out (or browned out or grayed out).
- Maybe a loved one asked you to not drink so much, and you got way more defensive than you should have.
- Maybe you've found yourself staying in more so you can start drinking earlier or don't have to worry about risking a DUI.
- Maybe you find yourself making both big and small decisions based on when, where, and how much you can drink.

Whatever it is, something led you to ask yourself the question, "Am I an alcoholic?" And if you're like me, you've either refused to answer it or you haven't answered it honestly. But here's the truth: Up until recently, I actually *couldn't* answer that question honestly. Not just because I was actively trying to ignore what my gut, my conscience, and the Holy Spirit were telling me but because I had a fundamental misunderstanding of what an alcoholic is.

That's one of the biggest problems facing us today. We don't actually understand what an alcoholic is—or what alcoholism is. Sometimes purposefully, sure, but a lot of times by no fault of our own. That's why this chapter is located here. In the end, I think what a lot of us have been told growing up about alcoholism is a lie, a misunderstanding, or a caricature.

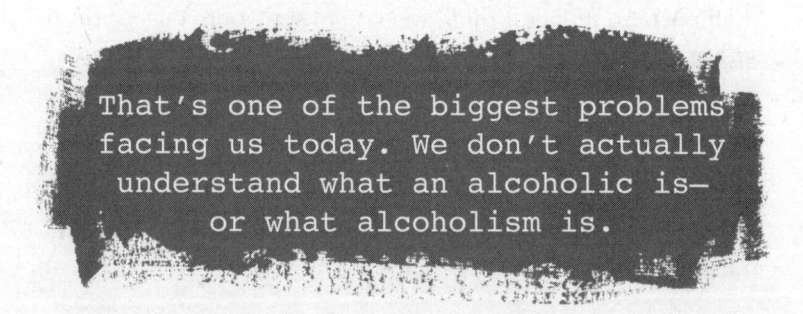

> That's one of the biggest problems facing us today. We don't actually understand what an alcoholic is— or what alcoholism is.

There are a lot of things working against us to obscure what alcoholism truly looks like. Culture is accosting us, marketing is deceiving us, and Hollywood is blinding us. Oh, and then there are things like trauma, mental health, genes, and upbringing that factor in. And don't forget about the major spiritual aspects as well!

So we enter the race for sobriety with forty-five-pound dumbbells tied around our necks. Newsflash: There's no way we're running that race successfully. So we have to remove the weights—we have to understand what alcoholism really is—and we do that with truth.

A Little Experiment

Let's try something. I want you to take a moment and use your imagination. Clear your mind as much as you can. Maybe take a deep breath. I'd say close your eyes, but I need you to read what I'm about to say. (So maybe close them after you read the next little bit.) Now, take a mental snapshot of the person who traditionally comes to mind when you hear the word *alcoholic*.

What does that person physically look like?

What do they sound like?

What do they smell like?

Where are they located?

What are they wearing?

What are they doing?

Where are they going?

What do they have in their hand?

Got it?

There's a good chance you imagined some down-and-outer. Maybe someone who is frail, drunk, or sloppy. Disheveled. They're stumbling, wobbling, slurring, or vomiting. Maybe you imagined someone angry, someone passed out, or someone driving drunk. A partier or a barhopper. You may have even imagined someone who has completely alienated their family, who has chosen alcohol over everything and everyone. A person who is visibly depressed or has hit rock bottom in the worst imaginable way.

For a long time, I imagined an alcoholic to be some variation or amalgamation of those things. After all, that's how Hollywood portrays them. I thought it was someone who had the shakes when they tried to quit, someone who probably had been pulled over for DUI, or someone who left a wake of drunken destruction that would be clear to everyone. But whatever combination of those things they had or were, they were at minimum this: easily identifiable.

But here's the truth: While what I noted above describes *some* alcoholics, it doesn't describe *all* alcoholics. And in fact, I wonder if it doesn't even describe a *majority* of alcoholics. How do I know? Well, because I'm an alcoholic, and almost none of those things above describe me. In fact, when I started telling people I was giving up drinking, many of them were surprised.

"You doing it for health reasons?"

"Just taking a break, right?"

"For Sober October / Dry January?"

The point is, it wasn't obvious that I needed to take a break. I didn't look or act like a "traditional" alcoholic. And yet I was one. Undoubtedly. Full-blown. I'll get into the stories a little later, but know this: I was dependent on alcohol. At my worst, I thought about it from the moment I woke up in the morning until I was finally buzzed or drunk enough to forget about it, which ironically is part of why I drank—to give my mind a break from thinking about getting drunk and to escape the guilt of drinking so much. Go figure.

But up until the very end, I never actually considered myself an alcoholic. Why? Because I didn't look like what I had been told an alcoholic looked like. I didn't act—at least not in *every* way—how I had seen alcoholics act. Or at least how they were portrayed to act. In my mind, there was always someone worse, and while at times I was bad, at least I wasn't *that* person. At least I wasn't doing *that*, whatever *that* was.

We alcoholics do that a lot. We play the comparison game. It's a game as dangerous as Russian roulette. It's a game that gets us into so much trouble and then, once we're there, keeps us trapped. We create a checklist in our mind, and as long as we don't tick every box, we're good. All the while, the list keeps growing.

Here's the reality: You can drink less than me and be an alcoholic. I can drink more than you and *not* be an alcoholic. Or let me put it this way: There are people who drink less than I drank who are alcoholics, and there are people who drink more than I drank who aren't alcoholics. It's true. And before we go anywhere else, I need you to understand that. It's foundational to everything else you're going to read.

How can that be? Because alcoholism isn't just about how much you drink, it's about the place that alcohol occupies in your life. Yes, quantity plays a factor, but not as much as we've been conditioned to think. And the sooner you realize that, the sooner you will be on your way to gaining power over it.

So let's look at what alcoholism truly is. If you're willing to listen to truth, then read on. Fair warning, though: It may just change your life. And while that may be good, it's not always easy.

What the Manual Says

I need to take you on a little journey for a few minutes.

When it comes to disorders and "-isms," like alcoholism, there's a really important book that the medical community uses. Created by the American Psychiatric Association, it's called the *Diagnostic and Statistical Manual of Mental Disorders*, or *DSM* for short.

The first edition of the *DSM* was published in 1952, and new editions don't come out often. For starters, it's a heavy lift to update the massive book. And second, there's a lot of science and research that must be considered before a change is accepted and released.

But in 2013, a major update was made in the form of the *DSM-5*. The previous edition, the *DSM-IV*, was published in 1994. That means nearly twenty years elapsed between major updates to one of the medical community's sacred texts, for lack of a better term. That's a long time. That also means that any changes are noteworthy.

And noteworthy is exactly what the manual's section on alcoholism is in the *DSM-5* compared to the *DSM-IV*.

Here's the big headline: "Alcoholism," which is the colloquial term we all use, is now called "alcohol use disorder" (AUD), and it's no longer as binary as it once was. In fact, alcoholism now exists on a spectrum. What that means is that it's no longer about whether you are an alcohol abuser or not an alcohol abuser or whether you are alcohol dependent or not alcohol dependent (which were the two categories before). With the update, now those categories have been combined, and there are varying degrees of AUD, from mild to moderate to severe.

So why tell you all that? Because ever since the medical community began diagnosing alcoholism, and up until 2013, it did so using fairly black-and-white criteria: Answer one or more questions positively out of five in the first category, and you were an alcohol abuser. Answer three or more positively out of seven in a second category, and you were alcohol dependent. If you didn't meet that minimum standard in either, you were good.

Here's the problem with those two criteria: What about the people who didn't fit neatly into those categories? Or even worse, what if someone said yes to two of the questions in the second category and stopped there? Did that mean they were off the hook?

Traditionally, the answer was yes. And that was a problem because a lot of people who answered yes to some of those questions but not enough of them weren't "good" at all.

The 2013 *DSM* update meant to change that. And in changing the section on alcoholism, the manual admitted something important: There are way too many people who have a problem with alcohol that the old criteria weren't covering. And those people—and all those around them—were suffering because of it.

As the National Library of Medicine puts it, the old way of defining alcoholism created "diagnostic orphans," or "individuals who [had] two dependence symptoms and no abuse symptoms and therefore did not meet any diagnostic criteria."[1] The new way is much more clear-cut.*

Following is the new criteria for AUD released in 2013. It only takes the presence of two of these eleven criteria for your drinking to be considered being on the *spectrum* of a disorder. Meet two to three of them and your case is considered mild, meet four to five and your case is considered moderate, meet six or more and your case is considered severe.

> ### Alcohol Use Disorder Diagnostic Criteria
>
> A problematic pattern of alcohol use leading to clinically significant impairment or distress, as manifested by at least two of the following, occurring within a 12-month period:
>
> 1. Alcohol is often taken in larger amounts or over a longer period than was intended.
> 2. There is a persistent desire or unsuccessful efforts to cut down or control alcohol use.

---

* The *DSM* isn't without its critics, both inside the church and outside of it. (See Jonathan K. Okinaga's book *From Sin to Disease*.) But no matter your thoughts on the manual, the important point is that a change in definition has occurred—and I believe we can use that change to our benefit.

3. A great deal of time is spent in activities necessary to obtain alcohol, use alcohol, or recover from its effects.
4. Craving, or a strong desire or urge to use alcohol.
5. Recurrent alcohol use resulting in a failure to fulfill rote obligations at work, school, or home.
6. Continued alcohol use despite having persistent or recurrent social or interpersonal problems caused or exacerbated by the effects of alcohol.
7. Important social, occupational, or recreational activities are given up or reduced because of alcohol use.
8. Recurrent alcohol use in situations in which it is physically hazardous.
9. Alcohol use is continued despite knowledge of having a persistent or recurrent physical or psychological problem that is likely to have been caused or exacerbated by alcohol.
10. Tolerance, as defined by either of the following:
    a. A need for markedly increased amounts of alcohol to achieve intoxication or desired effect
    b. A markedly diminished effect with continued use of the same amount of alcohol.
11. Withdrawal, as manifested by either of the following:
    a. The characteristic withdrawal syndrome for alcohol (refer to Criteria A and B of the criteria set for alcohol withdrawal in the DSM-5-TR).
    b. Alcohol (or a closely related substance, such as a benzodiazepine) is taken to relieve or avoid withdrawal symptoms.

Reprinted with permission from the *Diagnostic and Statistical Manual of Mental Disorders*, Fifth Edition, Text Revision (Copyright © 2022), American Psychiatric Association, 553–54. All rights reserved.

As for the withdrawal symptoms in number 11, they can range from nausea and vomiting to tremors ("the shakes"), to sweating, to headaches and anxiety, or even to hallucinations, just to name a few.[2]

"Reading through [the new AUD] list might feel terrifying," faith-based sobriety advocate Erin Jean Warde writes about the updated criteria, "but it offers some good news because it means we can begin to help people when they are in the mild and moderate stages of AUD rather than waiting to offer support until someone reaches severe AUD."[3]

Here's why that's important: On the night I finally got to the end of myself on the beach in Miami, would I have checked the appropriate boxes for alcohol dependence in the old criteria? No question. But a year earlier? Six months earlier? Nope. And yet, I still had a problem—a problem that I was partly able to justify because of my old understanding of alcoholism. An understanding that the old criteria helped perpetuate.

Simply put, I carried on for a long time with what is now medically considered a disordered relationship with alcohol. And I don't want that for you. The new criteria, the new understanding, makes it easier to identify a problem sooner.

Think of it this way: If we woke up tomorrow and found out there was a way to detect all cancer six months sooner, we'd be jumping for joy. And while I can't put a number on what this new way of looking at alcoholism does—maybe it's different for everyone—what I can say is that we should approach this new criteria, this new information, this new truth, with that same kind of hypothetical joy.

Don't get me wrong; I'm not saying that just because we're armed with this knowledge, alcohol use disorder will magically plummet and people like me won't struggle to give it up. We're going to cover later how it takes a lot more than knowledge to break free. But I am saying that I think it helps. I am saying that we now have an early warning siren. Whether we listen to that siren, cover our ears, or ignore it altogether is something different. But now we at least have it.

Maybe that's hard for you to see right now. Maybe you don't *want* to be told you might have alcohol use disorder, even if it's mild. I get it. It's going to be tough to swallow, unlike whatever your drink of choice is. But I'm telling you, it might just save your life, your family, your relationships, or your job.

And you'll thank me for that later.

Misordered Is Disordered

I said earlier that alcoholism (or alcohol use disorder, as it's now officially called) isn't about how much you drink, or at least not about quantity as much as you think. It's about the place alcohol occupies in your life. I didn't come up with that idea myself. The first person to tell me that was a recovering alcoholic named Aaron.

I met him while writing a story about how his chance encounter on a beach in Hawaii with a thirteen-year-old who had cancer changed his life. Aaron was an alcoholic at the time, but after meeting "the boy on the beach," as he called him, he found God and he found sobriety. While interviewing him for the article, I mentioned that I had recently started my own sobriety journey. I must have said something about quantity, because he quickly corrected me: "It's not about the amount, man."

If you look at the list of criteria from the *DSM-5*, Aaron is right. They're not solely about quantity. That tells us something.

What does it tell us exactly? Alcohol use disorder is alcohol use that's out of order. It's when alcohol occupies a more important role in your life than it should. It's when alcohol is misordered in your life. That understanding covers both the quantity of alcohol in your life *and* the quality of your life because of alcohol.

But Jon, I'm not getting drunk all the time! Again, this isn't just about quantity. While, near the end, I was getting drunk almost every night, that wasn't always the case. And yet I still had a problem when I wasn't. Sure, I wasn't *constantly* drunk, but as Brett would later say, I was living in a state of buzzed apathy. My quality of life was plummeting because of alcohol.

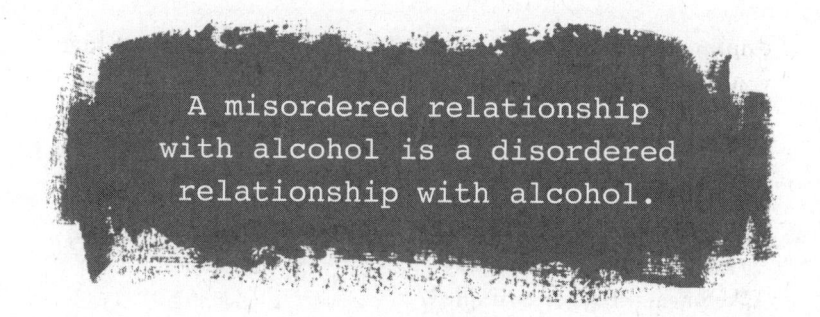

> **A misordered relationship with alcohol is a disordered relationship with alcohol.**

We spend a lot of time trying to figure out if we have a disordered relationship with alcohol, all the while ignoring the fact that a misordered relationship with alcohol *is* a disordered relationship with alcohol.

Let me say that again: A misordered relationship with alcohol *is* a disordered relationship with alcohol.

Ask yourself these questions about alcohol:

- Does it occupy your thoughts on a consistent basis?
- Do you make decisions—both big and small—based on it?
- Does it cause you to miss out on things?
- How much money are you spending on it?
- Does "treating yourself" generally involve alcohol?
- Does coping or escaping generally involve alcohol?
- Are you arguing with others about it?
- Are you drinking less, the same, or more than this time last year?
- Do you feel incomplete if you don't have a drink?
- How much brain power are you using to justify it or cover it up?

I could go on and on with these questions. And if you're struggling, and you're honest, your answers may make you a little uncomfortable.

But Jon, you're being even more strict than the medical handbook! you may be saying, or some variation of that.

I really don't think I am. I think the misordered = disordered idea is actually the *heart* of the *DSM-5* we mentioned earlier. It's the meaning behind the message. And in fact, the misordered/disordered designation is at the core of so many other disorders.

Take my anxiety, for example.

As I explain in my book *Finding Rest*, everyone has anxiety. Anxiety is simply a fight-or-flight response. It's a good thing meant to keep us alive. But an anxiety *disorder* is when your fight-or-flight response kicks in too often or at the wrong times. It's when fear occupies a misordered place in your life. Instead of keeping you alive, it starts interrupting your day-to-day functions and destroying your life.

In other words, my regular anxiety becomes an anxiety disorder when fear occupies a place of too much prominence in my life.

Doesn't that sound like what alcohol use disorder does?

This misordered/disordered way of looking at alcohol is also important because it keeps us from playing the comparison game. It's all about *your* personal relationship with alcohol, not about what someone else is doing or not doing and not about the number of drinks. You can't say, "Well, at least I'm not doing *that*." Another person's "that" doesn't matter. It's about where *you* are at. And you can't say, "Well, I'm not getting drunk." It's not even about drunkenness; it's about how you view alcohol and its place in your life.

It's also why I can say this: You don't need a "rock-bottom" moment to realize you need to cut back on, or give up, alcohol. I think that's a misunderstanding. Listen, I *wish* I hadn't had my moment in Miami. I *wish* I would have avoided that pain and heartache. And if I'd understood, embraced, and heeded the misordered/disordered early warning signs, I may not have.

Rock bottom is a sign that you need to change, sure. But it's unfortunately one of the last ones. There are plenty of others before you get to that point. And life will be less difficult if you recognize them.

What the Bible Says

When it comes to the misordered/disordered test, it doesn't just apply to the physical or emotional aspect of our lives. For Christians, there's a third one that's even more important: the spiritual aspect.

This isn't a popular thing to say these days—sometimes even among Christians, I've learned.* But it's true. Even if you reject everything I've said up to this point—the medical manual, my experience, the examples—if you're a Christian, there's one thing you can't deny. It's absolutely fundamental to orthodox Christian teaching, and it's fairly simple: Anything we elevate above God in our lives is sin, even the good things he gives us. When we want the gifts more than the Giver or when we worship the creation over the Creator, we are living in sin.

You know what that is? It's a misordered relationship. God both desires and commands us to put him first in our lives (see Matt. 6:33; Mark 12:30; Luke 4:8; Eph. 5:1–2; and Col. 3:1–2, just to name a few verses). When we don't—when we put other things first and disobey what he tells us about them—it's sin.

"When we give anything more priority than we give to God, we commit idolatry," Brennan Manning, author of *The Ragamuffin Gospel* and one of the most famous Christian alcoholics, explains. "Thus we all commit idolatry countless times every day."[4]

---

* Suffice it to say that people of all different backgrounds and persuasions are very opinionated when it comes to addiction recovery. I think that's partly why Christian strugglers are so shy about talking about their issues.

This is similar to what St. Augustine said so long ago in several of his classic works, that the root of so many of our problems comes down to disordered loves. In other words, when what we *should* love falls below what we *do* love, it creates havoc in our lives. We fall short. We are torn. We sin. That's what misordered/disordered comes down to. And that certainly sounds a lot like what became of my love for alcohol.

Besides that, the Bible is very clear about getting drunk. Newsflash: We shouldn't do it (Gal. 5:19–21). So if we are getting drunk, we're giving alcohol a bigger role in our life than God says we should. We're elevating it above obedience to him.

If you can justify everything else—if you can convince yourself that the way you use or view alcohol isn't out of order—but yet you call yourself a Christian and are still getting drunk, your relationship with alcohol is clearly misordered, disordered, and sinful. I'm sorry, but it just is. *Everything* we do should be done to the glory of God. And, in fact, Paul even says that applies to our eating and drinking (1 Cor. 10:31).*

So let me ask you: Are you drinking in a way that brings God glory?

But let me take it a step further: Maybe you're not getting drunk, and yet you feel a conviction to stop drinking, but you keep doing it. Guess what, as James 4:17 tells us, "Whoever knows the right thing to do and fails to do it, for him it is sin."

That's Kaiti's story. Kaiti, a young mom who was teacher of the year in her school district, told me how she started becoming convicted about her every-evening wine use. Even though she wasn't getting drunk, she realized it was occupying a misordered place in her life. She thought about it, she looked forward to it, and she made numerous decisions centered around if and when she could drink. It was her comfort. She was disappointed and even angry if

---

* That same chapter also says that just because something is "lawful" doesn't mean it's "helpful" (v. 23).

she didn't get her daily two glasses. After ignoring the conviction to quit for years, she finally gave it up.

She passed the "drunkenness test," but she failed the "conviction test."

Now, that doesn't mean you can't find ways to justify your drinking so that you can feel better and tell yourself it's not sinful. I did. For a long time, I called getting drunk "a little too buzzed" or "just tipsy," for example. Or, as I mentioned in the introduction, I told myself I wasn't really getting drunk because I wasn't having blackouts. Or I said something like, "Yeah, gluttony is a sin, but we all overeat every once in a while. Same thing with drinking, right? I'm not doing it *that* often."* Or how about this one: "Everyone has their struggles, sins, and vices. This is mine. No one is perfect!"

But I knew. You know. We all know at some point.

The harsh and sad reality is that I loved what alcohol gave me more than what Jesus was offering me. And more than a disorder of the body, that was a disorder of the soul.

And I suffered the consequences.

In Conclusion, It's Your Conclusion

As we wrap up this chapter, I want to be abundantly clear about something: I'm not trying to convince you you're an alcoholic, that you have alcohol use disorder, or that your relationship with alcohol is misordered/disordered. Trust me, your life is much better if none of those are true! And in fact, I'm not even saying that in all cases everyone should abstain completely from alcohol forever. I know Christians who have confronted a misordered/disordered relationship with alcohol who are now able to enjoy it responsibly.

---

* By the way, just because you may have a misordered/disordered relationship with food, it doesn't give you justification to have a misordered/disordered relationship with other things, especially alcohol.

It's not a lot of them, and it's not me, but it is possible. However, you need to be *really* honest with yourself about your tendencies, your struggles, and your convictions. I know the only drink I can say no to is the first one, so I abstain completely. Additionally, you can definitely still be a Christian and drink alcohol. I know plenty of them and hang out with them.*

Instead, what I am trying to show you is twofold. First, that "alcoholic" is really not the best way to describe what I am. I know, I use it in the title. But it got your attention, right?† I think there are times and places for the term, then, but I also think it's nuanced. Just know that it can lend itself to old understandings and incorrect mental images.‡

And that leads to the second thing I'm trying to show you: Instead of focusing on the quantity of our drinking, we really have to focus on our *relationship* with alcohol to figure out if we have a problem.

Not surprisingly, then, when you look at what alcohol use disorder actually is, I think more of us have a clinically misordered/disordered relationship with it than we want to admit—even if we're not getting drunk regularly, racking up DUIs, fighting the shakes, or "craving" it. And when you factor in the spiritual component of placing our comfort and escapism above what God calls us to do, the litmus test becomes even more damning.

In other words, not only are there a lot of us who fail the clinical test, but I think there are plenty more of us who fail the spiritual test when it comes to alcohol.

---

　* The Bible also doesn't teach complete abstinence for everyone. We see Jesus drinking wine, and Paul even tells Timothy to do so in 1 Timothy 5:23.

　† *Confessions of a Christian with Alcohol Use Disorder* just isn't really that catchy. But also, I now have a better understanding of the term and what it *should* mean, which is all about the AUD spectrum.

　‡ We can have *parts* of ourselves that act a certain way or desire a certain thing, and yet that doesn't mean we are *completely* whatever that desire or thing is. In other words, I have an "alcoholic" part, but that's not the whole of who I am. That will make sense if you keep reading.

In the end, though, you have to come to your own conclusion about your relationship with alcohol and then what to do about that. My main prayer is that you'll be open to whatever the Holy Spirit is telling you. Because if you're reading this, I have a sneaking suspicion that maybe, just maybe, he's trying to tell you something.

If he is, or even if you simply suspect he might be, there's plenty more waiting for you in the pages ahead. Most of all, there's hope. You aren't too far gone. You haven't committed the unpardonable sin. Not only can God still use you, he actually is. Right now.* How do I know? Well, that's what the rest of the chapters in this section are all about to some degree.

There's darkness, but there's also light.

However, for you to fully appreciate the light in my life, I need to show you how dark it actually got. And that's where we're headed next, into the pitch-black cavern of my story.

---

* Although you're not being used to your full potential, and you're not as fulfilled, joyful, and peaceful as you could be!

THREE

A Slow Fade

> Our spiritual sickness happens gradually over a period of time—a simple drift, a small deception, a tiny compromise, and suddenly we've turned away from the most important thing.
>
> —Matt Chandler, *The Overcomers*

I was sitting in a coffee shop across from an old friend I hadn't seen in years. He was in town for a conference and had reached out to catch up. He happens to be a recovering alcoholic as well.

We were the first to arrive as the baristas cracked the window shades and turned on the neon "open" sign. As the smell of fresh coffee grounds wafted through the air and early-morning commuters gave way to moms in yoga pants, I told him the story of the previous year.

I talked about Georgia, about Miami, about the ocean. I told him about the relapse and then the steady transformation. And then I told him a few other stories—stories that highlight just how bad my drinking got. I didn't tell him those stories because I'm proud of them. I told him those stories because I believe strongly that in order to appreciate where I am now, it's important to understand the depths of where I was. And at some points, I was twenty thousand leagues under the sea.

I want to do the same thing with you, here, right now.

That means the rest of this chapter is hard for me. Hard for me to write, hard for me to read, hard for me to recall—not because the details are fuzzy but because it requires dredging up a lot of things I tried to justify and don't love thinking about. One of the most painful parts is realizing that I missed so much—so much of my wife, my kids, and myself. But while I may have in some ways wasted those fifteen years of my life (ages twenty-one to thirty-six), God told me he was going to redeem the next fifteen. He is a God of redemption, after all. Of stories and of time.

So I want to do this. I need to do this. If I'm asking you to do the hard thing, you should see me do the hard thing, no matter how hard it is.

Here's what you need to know about my story, though. My slide wasn't all at once. It was little compromise after little compromise, small justification after small justification. A slow fade. Drinking wasn't my problem; drinking was the solution to my problems. Think about that. That's what I learned at deer camp, and it stayed with me for most of my life.

Because of that, you should also know this: There are more stories of darkness than what I can include here. I've picked the

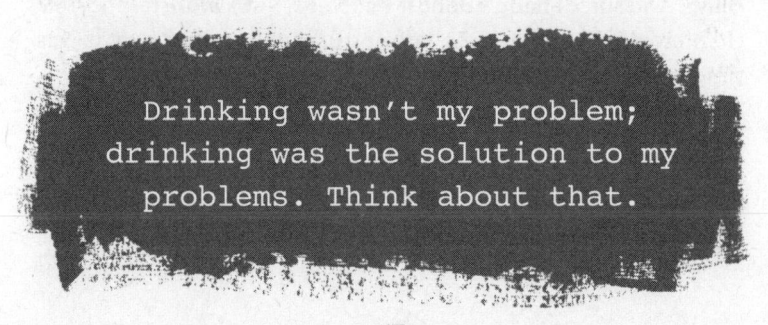

> Drinking wasn't my problem; drinking was the solution to my problems. Think about that.

"lowlights" for you. But what John's Gospel says about Jesus applies to my own drunken escapades: "Now there are also many other things. . . . Were every one of them to be written, I suppose that the world itself could not contain the books that would be written" (John 21:25).

Brooklyn

The idea that I became a Christian alcoholic is in some ways confusing to me. Despite deer camp and despite knowing what alcohol could do for me, that moment scared me. I catastrophize, and I always feared getting drunk would make me do something I would regret. I'm also a people pleaser. In fact, I once ratted myself out to my Christian college authorities for simply having some drinks underage (but legally) with my parents while on Christmas break.

But after I turned twenty-one in 2008, during my junior year of college in New York City, I made a decision: I was going to lighten up and live a little more. My anxiety made me too uptight. I was always striving, always worried about pleasing my professors. I found my value in the 4.0 semesters I was able to grind out. So I returned to deer camp.

That looked like visits with friends to a pizza place in New York's famed Penn Station that sold 32 oz. beers for $2.75. We'd take full advantage of the price, getting tipsy whenever we went. In my mind, I justified it by saying I didn't do it *that* often. I wasn't like the drunk homeless guys who were in the corner doing the same thing. And since I hadn't done it underage, I was *more* responsible than most.* I had been the good, studious kid, and now it was time to reward myself a little.

It wasn't long before the "treat" turned into gorging myself.

---

* The comparisons that would keep me trapped for years started early on, as you can see.

During my senior year of college, I signed a lease with six other guys for a three-bedroom apartment in Brooklyn. A rough part of Brooklyn, where the local Popeye's chicken restaurant was encased in bulletproof glass, and the bodega around the corner sold off-brand cigarettes by the singles and 24 oz. regular Coors for a dollar.

It's not an exaggeration to say that we escaped with our lives. In fact, we had one roommate who almost didn't. While boarding the subway train near our apartment one fall morning, a homeless man chased him with a piece of rebar, attempting to bludgeon him because he didn't like the way our roommate rushed by him. Shortly after, that roommate threw all his clothes into a trash bag and left like a thief in the night. He spent the rest of the school year living on someone's couch. It was safer and less stressful.

Another time, a different roommate had just returned from the laundromat at 11:00 a.m. on a Saturday when we heard a *pop, pop, pop*. We looked out the window and realized that someone had shot up a parked car in front of our apartment. Just because.

And then there was the evening some visiting friends were steps away from the bodega on their way to get some beer when someone came out firing a gun in the air like Yosemite Sam. I'm telling you, this place was a gem.*

On top of all that, while Brett and I were engaged at the time, we had been dating long-distance for nearly two years after she transferred from my college, where we met, to a university in Denver. That spring—the spring before our wedding—she chose to do a study-abroad program in Latin America. FaceTime didn't exist. International cell phone service wasn't an option where she was going. And the best we could do was buy a bunch of calling cards and try to maintain our relationship over the course of minutes-long conversations every week, if we were lucky. She would return

---

* The irony in all this is that the area was soon gentrified and turned into a hipster haven.

from the trip, and we would have just weeks to fully prepare ourselves for the wedding.

How do you handle all that? That stress. That fear. Those emotions.

I returned to deer camp. To the relief that Carlo Rossi gave me on that December evening. Not necessarily consciously. I don't think for us unhealthy drinkers it always is. Sometimes the habits are like alcoholic aberrations we can't fully make out but know are there. My body, my mind, as Dr. Bessel van der Kolk brilliantly outlines in his book *The Body Keeps the Score*, remembered.

So, as a broke college student, I took the easiest, most cost-effective route, which was also the unhealthiest: I began drinking. A lot. All six of us started drinking. A lot. As one of my old roommates from that era told me recently, "It was one of the most stressful environments imaginable, and we dealt with it through cheap relief."

Boy, did we ever.

I remember throwing up on the subway platform immediately after peeing on the tracks late one night when we actually braved the neighborhood and ventured out to a brewery. I didn't have enough money to pay for beer, so one roommate offered to buy me two when we got there and gave me a small bottle of cheap vodka to "pregame" at the apartment. I did, and paid the price.

I remember too many late-night drunken runs to "Pie-pies," as one wasted roommate once called the fried-chicken joint, forever solidifying it into lore. And I remember one of our other roommates, who was a budding photographer, taking Brett's and my engagement photos in Central Park while so hungover he was late to the shoot.

In other words, we were an anxious group, in an anxious place, where the only safe form of entertainment was also the cheapest: We'd pool our money, go down to the bodega, buy a bunch of one-dollar beers, and play Mario Kart on N64 for hours. It was epic, fun, and fiscally responsible, we told ourselves. And we weren't doing anything "stupid" like other, normal college students.

So we lined the apartment with liquor bottles and beer cans from our nights in. For a year, they stood like monuments to each weekend we survived. We weren't smart enough to wash them out before we set them up, though, meaning many of the beer cans were growing mold we didn't know about. What a perfect metaphor for what we were doing to ourselves.

How perfect? At least three of us (that I know of) developed unhealthy relationships with alcohol later in life. We got a lot of practice in numbing our emotions. In escaping with alcohol. In masking what we were feeling. It's also where my "drinking style," so to speak, started to develop: I'm not a party drinker; I'm not a barhopper; I'm not a stay-out-late drinker. I'm a safe-haven drinker. I'm a chug-to-shut-my-mind-off drinker. I'm a these-thoughts-won't-stop-and-these-feelings-are-hard drinker. I'm a sit-in-the-apartment-or-house-and-be-safe drinker. And that emerged during our stressful year in Brooklyn.

It wouldn't come back to haunt me immediately, though.

Too Broke to Drink

After graduation and leaving Brooklyn, I married Brett and moved to Denver. She was a year behind me and had two more semesters to complete before graduation. I took a job as an admissions counselor for the Adult and Graduate Studies department of her school.

And I barely drank.

The journey to a drinking disorder can take twists and turns, just like the journey to addiction recovery. And that was true for me on more than one occasion. Being newly married, and with Brett still in school, I'm not exaggerating when I say we were broke. People romanticize living in Colorado and assume you're always skiing, biking, or doing something outdoors. But you know what? Those things cost money. And we had none of it. We never went skiing, we took maybe one trip to Rocky Mountain National Park, and we used a cash-envelope budget to track our expenses.

In other words, I couldn't afford to get drunk.

But there was also a desire not to show Brett *that* side of me. She wasn't around for the Brooklyn year, and I didn't offer her details. After all, she had a much different upbringing with alcohol than I did. So much so that our first big fight was about alcohol at our wedding. She had a family full of traditional Southern Baptists in her home state of Texas, the kind who believed that sex could lead to dancing. (Read that again.) But my family? Drinking at a wedding is pretty much required, no matter how Christian you are or aren't. That's the Wisconsin way.

"I can't invite my Wisconsin family down to a wedding in Texas and not offer them something to drink," I said. "It would be a slap in the face."

My soon-to-be father-in-law was baffled. But to his credit, he called a pastor friend in Wisconsin and asked him if "the whole alcohol thing" really was as big a deal as I was making it.

"Brian," the pastor told him bluntly, "not having alcohol at a wedding in Wisconsin is like not having a bride."

That settled it. But we still compromised: My dad purchased champagne and wine for the reception, and I promised not to drink at all as a sign of respect for Brett's family.* For our toast, we filled the champagne flutes with milk as an ode to America's Dairyland. No lie.

But even back then, I showed signs of slipping—of compromising—when it came to alcohol.

---

* The wedding program, though, had to specifically say that *my* family had provided the alcohol, to keep the peace.

If I'm honest, I was disappointed that I couldn't drink at my own wedding. I wanted to so badly. So much so that, at one point late in the reception, I picked up a champagne flute and started sipping it. Brett saw me and very pointedly reminded me of my promise. I put it down, defeated. And it was there, in the first hours of our marriage, that Brett's propensity to remind me of my promises around alcohol began. And so did my propensity to break them.

After that, though, I can think of a handful of times I was able to afford alcohol during our nine months living in the Denver area. And I never once got drunk. Instead of "too big to fail," I was "too broke to drink."

I'd start making up for it soon enough.

The Late New York Years

In the spring of 2010, knowing she was about to graduate, Brett got an itch to return to New York City. While she had only spent one year there, she loved it. The architecture, the pace, the people, the opportunities. Me? I like to say I went to college *despite* the city, not because of it. I'm more at home with a fifth in the woods than on Fifth Avenue. But she was insistent, in a good way.

So I told her that if I could find a good job, we'd move. Lo and behold, I used my politics, philosophy, and economics degree to land a gig at a prestigious policy institute. We moved, taking over the lease of a one-bedroom, garden-level apartment in Queens from some old friends of ours, sight unseen.

And it was awful. I mean, awful.

For starters, the apartment was infested with cockroaches. You'd open a cupboard and they'd start running out. It was also dark and wet, which led to mold growing on the walls. And we had only one small window air conditioner that we put in our bedroom for the sweltering, dank New York summer so we could attempt to sleep.

And the job at the prestigious policy institute? That was awful too. It wasn't at all what I had imagined. I was constantly berated, belittled, and treated like a commodity by my boss. I was once chided for not answering an email that came in at 5:00 a.m.—and this was before everyone had a smartphone. The overall work and mission of the organization was great, but I tell people that my boss was the political version of Meryl Streep in *The Devil Wears Prada*.

It's the first time in my life that I can recall a severe bout of depression taking over, and it started one week into the new job. I remember walking past Grand Central Station and asking myself through tears, *What have you done?*

I immediately started putting out feelers for another job. But I also returned to deer camp. I returned to the apartment in Brooklyn. I returned to alcohol.

Since Brett and I were both working (she had found a job at a Christian nonprofit, using her degree in biblical studies), we had a little more money. Not a ton but a little. We could afford to do things like eat out, and I was always sure to get a beer with dinner. As big of one as I could. And I drank wine. A lot of wine.

There's a culture in New York City that's just different, especially when it comes to drinking and wine, even among Christians. During the time we spent there together, we were always buying wine. For everything. Whenever you went to someone else's apartment, you brought wine. Whenever you met up for an afternoon in the park, you brought wine. And when you got together with your weekly church small group, *everyone* brought wine.

You drank during weekday lunches, you drank during dinners, and you drank during every gathering. And it was all done under the guise of East Coast sophistication. You shouldn't binge beers, but you could cuddle a cabernet. It's just what you did, no matter if you loved Jesus or hated Christians. And don't get me started on the boozy, all-you-can-drink brunches.

It was just what my sinful, anxious, depressed nature needed as an excuse. Add in the fact that you never had to worry about driving anywhere, and I took full advantage. We always had a bottle of wine or two in the apartment, we always had access to it at friends' places, and I always had a full glass.

Day Drinking

Within a few months of moving back to NYC, I caught my break, so to speak. Through contacts at my alma mater, I was introduced to someone who was leading a news start-up. He was looking for writers, and I had a background in journalism. By my final year of college, I had interned at a magazine, had my own column in the school newspaper, and had a dream of someday writing for a living.

So in late summer of 2010, I quit the worst job I've still ever had at the policy institute and signed on as the first writing hire of a new digital news organization. And we broke the internet. No, really. We did more traffic on our first day than we thought we'd do in our first month, and the site crashed. From there, it just got wilder and more successful.

But as it often does, success breeds stress.

I could say a lot of things about the craziness of the 24/7 news cycle, but I'll say this: It's hustle culture on steroids. It's constant, and you're only as good as your next story. It chews you up and spits you out, especially when you're doing it in the news capital of the world, New York City. You have to do more and more to get ahead, more and more to just keep up, and give more and more tomorrow than you gave yesterday. And even that is rarely enough. It requires you to suppress parts of yourself, and those parts of you die. If you're lucky enough, you can revive them once you get out. But not everyone is that lucky. I still wonder if I've lost some parts of myself forever.

So I returned to deer camp and drank to deal with it. And then I drank some more. And I developed a schedule that allowed me to do just that. See, I'm sharpest in the mornings, so I volunteered to take the "early shift" of running the site. In general, my hours were 7:00 a.m. to 3:00 p.m., but that was more of a suggestion. There was always another story. There was always another video. There was always more I could do. So I did it. I didn't want to just impress my boss; I wanted to impress my boss's bosses.

But instead of working later to make that happen, I worked earlier. Why? Because I wanted to protect my 3:00 p.m. quit time. Why was *that* so important? Because it meant I could start drinking then. And drink as much as I wanted before Brett ever got home, usually around 6:00 p.m. In other words, I had about three hours to myself to decompress from the news of the day (which was often angry, awful, and agitating), slow my mind down, and just escape.

And I was in a place and culture that made that both accessible and acceptable.

So that's what I did. I had a few favorite restaurants in the area that I would visit for happy hour, which I thought was providence. My workday ended when happy hour began, meaning I could drink more for less. I quickly learned something important about my body: If I didn't eat before drinking, I'd feel the effects of the alcohol a lot stronger and a lot quicker. If I drank on an empty stomach, I'd be able to empty my mind much sooner, much easier, and actually much cheaper. *That's responsible, right?*

And that's what I did. Often. At this point, though, I was still cautious enough to hide it from Brett. That meant I'd spend the first two hours drinking, the last hour eating and sobering up, and when we'd finally meet up, I'd maybe be a little buzzed, but I'd tell her I only had a couple, along with an appetizer, to unwind.

The lying and hiding started early, in other words. And I got really good at it.

The Dallas Move

In the spring of 2012, Brett and I struck gold.

We knew we didn't want to live in NYC forever, and we knew we definitely didn't want to raise kids there.* All of Brett's immediate family had somehow ended up in the Dallas, Texas, area, and we'd visit for holidays and comment on how nice it was. "Maybe this is where we could raise a family," we both said at different times.

But how would that work? I was in the national news business, and the center of the national news business—not just for my company but for any company—was in New York City.

Then came the big surprise. My boss announced the founder of our company was moving the main headquarters to Dallas. Considering my status in the company (I had risen to managing editor), he wanted me to relocate to be the liaison and representative between the founder and the website. I'd get a bonus, the company would pay all our moving expenses, and I would essentially get a raise because there was no state income tax.

We were floored. We said yes and moved within a couple months. Quickly, we realized relocating to Dallas was as glorious as we thought it would be. However, it did come with an unintended consequence: The lower cost of living and more expendable income meant I could now afford to drink even more. A lot more. And it also meant that I was still working on East Coast time. Why was that important? Because now, instead of getting off at 3:00 p.m., I could get off at 2:00 p.m.—an extra hour to drink before Brett got home.

That extra hour also coincided with the national craft beer boom, and Dallas was at the center of it. Every day, a new craft brewery or new growler refill station was opening up nearby. Access was

---

* After a year in the roach-infested apartment, we did find another place that was much better, at least.

everywhere, and I fell in love with local brews that had funny names and high ABV content.

The apartment we moved into was the one with the pool where I would drink heavily on Sundays. Life was good. Or was it?

It was around this time that I first started becoming convicted about my drinking. Brett had also started softly mentioning things about cutting back or taking a break. Sometimes I would listen, but most times I would get defensive—with her and with myself. After all, for years I was able to justify what I was doing and how I was doing it, and I was a master at playing the comparison game:

- I'm not getting blackout drunk.
- I'm not drinking *during* work.
- I'm not drinking and driving.
- I'm actually a *better* husband by drinking and "taking the edge off."
- My job isn't suffering, and in fact, I'm *excelling*.
- It makes me real and relatable.
- I don't really go out to drink.
- I'm fighting back against legalism.
- I deserve it.
- It helps me.

But we had found a church with a pastor like none I had ever experienced before. He was real, loud, and expressive like me. He didn't pull punches, and he illuminated the Bible in new ways. I began growing deeper in my faith. But that also meant I began growing in something else: conviction. I became more and more aware of my destructive drinking.

But having conviction and listening to conviction are two different things. I think that's hard for some people to understand, but I think problem drinkers understand it perfectly well. And even the apostle Paul got it. "For I do not understand my own actions," he says in Romans 7:15. "For I do not do what I want, but I do the very thing I hate."

Talk about a life verse for me.

But as conviction grew, so did my ability to stifle it. Around the mid-2010s, though, my internal destruction started showing external cracks.

The Ramping Up (2014–2020)

By 2014, I had turned into an almost daily drinker. I'd get up early, work my butt off, and then unwind around 2:00 p.m. We were now renting a loft in downtown Dallas that had the Texas version of a New York bodega located on the first floor. And while there were no gunfights like in New York City, they did have cheap beer. Once again, I could restock without driving—and that helped me skirt accountability.

That said, I did cut back for a time. I got my official anxiety and OCD diagnosis during this period, and the doctor told me to limit my alcohol consumption. Out of fear, I did. Instead of drinking every day, I tried drinking only on the weekends, or maybe only drinking three days a week, or sometimes only drinking beer, or sometimes [*fill in the blank*].

I don't remember how long it lasted, but it didn't last long. It never lasted long. When we found out we were pregnant with our first child, we purchased a house in a northern suburb of Dallas, and with my own palace came new excuses. I could drink before, during, and after yard work. I could mix drinks for friends who wanted to see the house. I could drink to celebrate all the firsts and milestones. I could drink with neighbors.

Quickly, the daily drinking started again. And the question that I had worked hard to stifle years earlier began resurfacing: "Am I an alcoholic?" That question came roaring back around the time I was invited on a trip to Israel and one of the first thoughts in my head was, *What if you can't drink every day?* I quickly snuffed it out, though, mostly with more drinking. And when I didn't get the shakes after not imbibing every day on the trip, I took that as a sign that I didn't really have a problem.

I did have a problem; I just wasn't ready to admit it.

That said, I knew my anxiety was increasing despite my efforts to curtail it. So I did make one change: I left my job in the news business. I thought that maybe if I could cut the stress, I could cut the drinking. You know what? That was somewhat true. Like I said, my drinking journey is filled with twists and turns. And some of the worst justifications for continuing to drink and eventually getting to such a disastrous place were the times I could and did cut back.

See, I don't really have a problem, I'd tell myself.

I found a much slower-paced job helping lead a Christian nonprofit, and for about a year and a half, I drank somewhat less. There were still moments of drunkenness, don't get me wrong. But the volume of drinking was down, even if the consistency was still there.

My year and a half of somewhat mindful drinking eventually faded when I was recruited to work for a prominent Christian figure, overseeing his digital media efforts. I reported to people on the West Coast and East Coast, so for the most part I was by myself.

For a while, I worked in a coworking space where one of the perks was free draft beer. I started taking advantage of that regularly. But since there were other Christians in the office who knew who

I was and who I worked for, I would sneak away and put it in my coffee mug. Eventually, due to budget cuts, I had to end the lease on that workspace as well as lay off an employee. That was hard. Really hard. How did I deal with it? I ran back to deer camp. And that's when things really ratcheted up. I had no office, no watching eyes, and I was depressed. Factor in that I was essentially my own boss, and it was a recipe for disaster.

I soon found a pizza-and-beer place close to my house that served an ale I absolutely fell in love with. It had high alcohol content, a low(er) price, and it matched my flavor palate: slightly bitter but fruity. The managers and employees began to know me by name. I'd walk in, and by the time I sat down they'd already have one poured and in front of me. It wasn't long before my late-afternoon unwind sessions began getting earlier and earlier. Some days, I was even the joint's first customer, and if they brought me a beer without asking, who was I to turn it down, even if it was 10:30 a.m.?

I'll stack my calls in the morning and leave the busywork for the afternoons. And if I'm just doing mindless work, what's wrong with a little buzz to get through the monotony?

But nothing ever goes as planned for long when you're planning your drunkenness. Needless to say, I took more than a few unexpected calls in the afternoon while buzzed or drunk at the restaurant. And that means something else: There's no doubt now that if I had gotten pulled over driving home from many of those "work" sessions, I would have been ticketed for a DUI. I once had a cop following me for quite some time, and I was convinced that was it. A law enforcement friend had told me that, on average, someone drives drunk about seven times before they get their first DUI. I'm not sure what number I was on, but I was flirting with that. When I didn't get pulled over this particular time, it scared me straight for a while. You know, something like a week. That was a good break, right?*

---

* During this time, I'd regularly lie to Brett about having meetings or calls late in the afternoon so I didn't have to pick up our daughter (and later our son) from day care, giving me an excuse to drink instead.

> **Nothing ever goes as planned for long when you're planning your drunkenness.**

I went right back to pushing and exceeding the limits. Eventually, I even started rationalizing driving drunk.

What is drunk anyway? I can hold my beer better than most. I'm from Wisconsin! Even if I'm technically over the limit, I'm actually fine to drive. Regular drunk and Wisconsin drunk are two different things. If I were truly bad, I'd be swerving all over the place. And I'm actually more attentive after a few in me!

Those mental gymnastics were a turning point for me but not in a good way. That's because driving under the influence was always my Rubicon. I had told myself that I would never drive drunk. Never. If I had a problem, it was *my* problem, and I wasn't going to put anyone else at risk. Never.

But problem drinking turns our "I won't" into "just this once." It turns our "never" into "never again." It takes our "hell no" and turns it into our own little hell. It puts our Rubicon—our *Rubicons*—in the rearview mirror. And that was true for me.

By now, I was running toward the right side of the AUD spectrum like an Olympic sprinter chasing a gold medal and a world record.

There was the time we hosted old friends for dinner. I had started drinking while making the food because, well, making dinner was a great excuse to drink. Our friends ended up being late, and when they finally showed up, I was hammered. By the end of the night, I was telling them about Brett's and my sex life. I have no idea why. Brett was mortified and sent me to bed before they even left.

There was the night when, while I was on part-time staff at our church, we joined a few other couples for a limo ride through the ritzy part of Dallas to see Christmas lights. We were allowed to drink in the back, and I took full advantage. By the end of the evening, my almond-sized bladder needed relief and I was peeing in empty water bottles under a jacket. I thought I was being sneaky by dumping them out the window, but Brett and some others knew what I was doing. I justified it by saying I wasn't the *only* one who was "a little tipsy."

There were the times that, while serving as a church home-group leader, I would drink beforehand and lead the discussion either buzzed or coming off a buzz. I told myself I needed to wash away the worries of the day so I could be fully present for the group. *I'm actually doing them a favor!*

Then there was the time I was playing in a softball league, representing a family member's church team, no less. I had some time to kill before our game started, so I went to the gas station to pick up a beer. *All the other teams drink before and after, so why not me?* I downed forty-eight ounces of beer before taking the field—and still was only slightly buzzed. I did, however, get in an argument with the umpire and nearly got tossed from the game.

There was also the time I had given up drinking for Lent, only to fly to New Orleans to have some tests done because I was donating my kidney to a stranger.[*] I told myself I was doing something good and noble and deserved a few drinks at the airport bar. A few drinks turned into who knows how many, and I had to call my niece—who was living with us at the time—to come pick me up from the airport. I told her and Brett that they had run so many tests and taken so much blood, I was "just a little too

---

[*] That's a whole other book!

woozy to drive." We had to come pick my car up at the airport the next day.

Or how about the time I had been drinking Natural Lights most of the afternoon (during the week) and got a call from a friend. Halfway through the conversation, I threw up. I thought I had muted the phone, but in my drunkenness, I forgot to. I covered it up by saying I had a stomach bug.

And finally, there was the time I flew home to Wisconsin at a moment's notice because my stepdad had a stroke and was in the ICU. It wasn't looking good. While waiting for signs of life, I got drunk one night, no doubt to escape the emotions. My oldest brother, Jeremy, woke me up in the wee hours of the next morning to let me know we needed to go to the hospital to say goodbye. I was hung over as I watched him take his final breath.

There was no place I couldn't, or wouldn't, drink. No occasion too sacred. No moment too important. And that led to the severe-slide period.

The Severe Slide (2021-2023)

By 2021, I knew I had a problem. I wasn't ready to admit that out loud, but I knew. Deep down, I knew. Even while on writing retreats for my first book, *Finding Rest*, I would reward myself for accomplishing a lot by drinking all evening. I was aware enough of the growing problem to put a line in that book about watching how much I drank. I was watching it all right—but I was watching it spiral.

Then came autumn of 2021.

"You need to be careful, Jon," a friend told me right before *Finding Rest* debuted. "There's almost always a letdown after you publish a book. Books rarely do as well as we want them to, and so much of your life for the last eighteen months has been wrapped up in this project. You can struggle to find purpose after and feel a little lost."

Yeah right, I thought mockingly. I wasn't going to fall into that. I had trained for this, in a way. My mental health seemed to be in a good spot. I was taking the right steps. I had even cut back on my drinking in preparation for the book release. I was good.

Until I wasn't.

Even though my book became number one in several categories and broke the top one hundred on all of Amazon, I quickly realized I had unspoken dreams—dreams that, when they never materialized, tapped into some sinister lies that I now know past trauma had convinced me were true.

You're a failure. You're not good enough. No one wants you the way you are. How embarrassing.

I thought my email would be buzzing with speaking requests. They never came.

I thought I really had a chance at the *New York Times* Best Seller List, or at least the *USA Today* or *Wall Street Journal* ones. I didn't.

I thought the big publishing houses would come begging for more books with big contracts. They were silent.

So I started drinking more and more to mask the hurt of those unmet expectations. Every night. Not necessarily getting wasted, but definitely getting a buzz. And I started pulling back—from friends, from family, from community, from commitments.

The difficulty didn't end there, though. By this season, I had started working full-time on my own digital media consulting business. That carried enough stresses in and of itself that "required" regular drinking. But then, in December of 2021, I lost my biggest client, the client that was floating the entire business. Because of what they were paying me and the focus I had to give them, they were essentially my only account. But in an effort to cut expenses and with almost no notice before Christmas, I was told my contract was up at the end of the month. And just try finding new clients in late December and early January. It's impossible.

I was blindsided. I was devastated. And then I was bored. The timing of the loss meant I had a lot of time on my hands, and so I threw myself into the bottle. I started drinking earlier and earlier. I'd take whole "me" days, and "me" days always involved treating myself to craft beer and now my new obsession: bourbon. I realized I could get to the "good place" a lot quicker with stiff bourbon, and the evidence was even a little easier to hide—no noticeable cans.

But Jon, why didn't you follow the advice in your own book on what to do when you start feeling like this?

Because you can know the truth and not embody it. You can know what's best and not want to fight for it. Because what's best is often hard, and I wanted the easy way. Because I went back to deer camp, although deer camp had now been replaced by a thousand other examples of how alcohol could transport me away, just for a little bit, and help me escape the choking reality.

I limped along through most of 2022, especially after losing a big replacement client because of the faltering economy. I secured some smaller accounts, but nothing to the degree that I once had. I was scraping by, and I had to do more work at a lower price just to keep the money coming in. I questioned who I was. I doubted my worth and my value. More than once, I had to fight off suicidal thoughts. And then, on top of it all, doctors found a tumor in my young son's leg, which took longer than I would've liked to determine was benign.

I prayed it all away in the mornings and drank it all away in the evenings. And the cracks grew into caverns. I called bosses, friends, church leaders, and clients drunk. Almost nothing was off limits.

That "almost" part was dangerous. I convinced myself I still had standards, I had Rubicons I wouldn't cross, and as long as I didn't cross them, I didn't really have a problem.

That led me to a false-bottom moment in December 2022. False-bottom moments are those times that maybe ten or five or two years ago, you would have said were your rock bottom. But they come and go without much fanfare, and before you know it, they're not a giant Rubicon you've crossed but a creek you've barely noticed.*

On the weekday afternoon of my daughter's school Christmas program, I decided to have a bourbon. But as is my case, the only drink I can say no to is the first one. By the time the program started, I was several deep, and they were hefty pours. (My hand becomes a lead weight when pouring my own drinks.) During the program, which I was enjoying, Brett elbowed me and told me to stop singing along so loud. I was embarrassing her and starting to make a scene. I barked back and kept going.

Who does that? I thought the next day. *Who shows up drunk to their own daughter's elementary school Christmas program?*

Throughout this time, I started noticing something: Even though I wasn't getting blackout drunk, more and more I was waking up the next day with missing fragments. While I would remember Brett and I having conversations—sometimes important, sometimes even combative—I wouldn't remember what they had been about.

That's not blackout drunk! I remember we had the conversation, at least, I'd tell myself.

So I got smart: While I was drinking, and if we started having any sort of conversation, I would open the notes app on my phone and literally start typing what was going on. I'd write what I said, what she said, what I was happy about, what I was irritated about.

---

 * Remember, not everyone needs to have or will have a rock-bottom moment to change their relationship with alcohol. That belief is actually something that can keep people in a misordered/disordered relationship with alcohol a lot longer.

And then I'd review it, either later that night or the next morning, and commit the facts to memory. On more than one occasion, if I forgot to take notes, I'd wake up in the middle of the night in a panic, realizing that Brett and I had argued about something but I couldn't remember what it was about or the point I had been trying to make. I'd apologize the next day but be careful to do so in the most general terms possible.

I battled smaller waves of depression throughout this time, but then came the big one near the end of 2022. While I had pulled back from a lot of relationships in my life—or put on a front with those people and convinced them I was busy—I had one friend I talked to every morning, usually multiple times a day. We went on weekend retreats together, he encouraged me, and he kept me (somewhat) level.

I told everyone he was my best friend.

So when he came down with depression in October 2022, in many ways I was just plain screwed. Research shows that depression can actually be contagious.[1] Add in the closeness of our relationship, and it was an awful combination. There are several names for this, but I like "empathetic depression." I'm an empathetic person, so when my best friend got depressed, I literally felt and took on his emotions as my own. Add in my own issues, and my mental health absolutely plummeted.

What did I do? I drank. I drank alone, I drank often, and my friend and I drank together. There were more than a few occasions where we met for "work lunches" that stretched into the early evening and I had no business driving home. The words from my police officer friend would pop up in my head: *Someone drives drunk about seven times before they get their first DUI.* By now I knew I was well north of that and was just playing with fire.

A Slow Fade

The beginning of 2023 didn't make things better: I had a book deal fall through for reasons that have never been fully explained to me (although I know now it was God's providence), my wife's business hit a slowdown we never saw coming, and my work was drying up. The drinking increased, but it started to not be enough. That's when I tried other coping methods like Delta 8 gummies, the legal version of hemp that has exploded onto the scene. I'd mix them with alcohol until the screaming voices telling me what a failure I was stopped, at least for a few hours. And then I'd get up and do it again—earlier and earlier in the day.

Barely anybody knew. Brett had an inkling, but she didn't know what to do. She prayed. And prayed. And prayed some more. I also hid it well from her. For example, she and I share our phone locations with each other, and on afternoons when I didn't have much work and started drinking early, I would check where she was—especially toward the end of the day—so I could down a few more and then have time to hide the evidence. Part of me wanted to stop. But when that part got too loud or too serious, I would either tell myself, *Just one more time*, or I would drink that part into silence. The lying, the hiding, the cycles of shame were all growing.

I yearned to escape. To get away. To return to deer camp. And I did, to the detriment of my soul and my family—flushing away parts of myself with each trip to the bathroom to get rid of the temporary relief. I had gone from a gregarious extrovert to a self-centered hermit. So many times, Brett would make comments like, "You've become kind of a homebody now." Of course I had, because at my worst, my life had become so much about me and what I wanted and what I told myself I deserved.

By the end, I was basing so many decisions on how *much* I could drink, *when* I could drink, and *where* I could drink—and all those decisions put *my* wants at the forefront. If I had started drinking in the late afternoon and Brett wanted to go out to dinner as a family, I would make up some excuse (or just flat-out say I didn't want to go) because I knew that either I wasn't in any shape to venture out, or I was so focused on getting to that point as soon as possible and didn't want the interruption.

Did I feel bad about that? Of course. But oftentimes I would project the anger and disappointment I had with myself onto Brett. The number of fights I'd pick with her during my drinking that were really aimed at myself was alarming. It's like I had to try and make dirty what I saw clean because dirty people like others to be dirty around them. Brett—this beautiful, gracious, long-suffering woman who dealt with her emotions in a healthy way—was like a mirror reflecting how poorly I did all those things. So I'd try to fog up the mirror. I'd nitpick. I'd find things to point out that *she* was doing wrong. All because I was disgusted with myself.

"We get defensive with others when we feel at odds with ourselves," licensed Christian counselor Dr. Alison Cook explains in her important book *I Shouldn't Feel This Way*.[2] I gave a master class on that.

In the end, alcohol is one of the most expensive and twisted tenants we allow to rent room in our bodies. And the relationship is all backward. We pay *it* to stay the night, and then we oddly thank it for leaving the carpets and the walls destroyed. We clean up its mess on our hands and knees and then invite it back for another stay. And another. And another. It literally abuses our bodies, and we ask for more. We think we're using it, but it's really just ruling us.

That finally came to a head on the Miami trip. My slow fade, which had become a sprint toward the death of so much of me, had been exposed. And I was finally willing to let Jesus shine a light onto every part of my dark soul, face the monsters lurking in the shadows, and embrace sobriety.

PART 2

MAKING SENSE OF IT

FOUR

How Does This Happen?

> We're always the last to know the person in the mirror.
> —David Powlison, *How Does Sanctification Work?*

> Author's note: This chapter is helpful for the person struggling with a misordered/disordered relationship, but it is also helpful for the friend or loved one of a struggling person.

My wife tells me I have a special relationship with my daughter. But the truth is, she doesn't have to convince me.

I love being a girl dad to our oldest child, Annie. And from what I can tell, she loves it too. In fact, she started a special ritual she calls "talk time."* That's when, after Brett and I tuck her in at night, she asks me to stay so we can chat about whatever is on her mind.

---

* I also absolutely love being a boy dad. And as my son, Jack, gets older, I'm discovering our own special relationship. He's even started asking for his own talk time.

Some nights it's school.

Some nights it's friends.

Some nights it's outer space.

Some nights it's dogs.

Some nights it's Jesus.

Some nights it's good.

Some nights it's bad.

But most nights the routine is that I lie down beside her, put my arm under her head, and we talk as the moonlight illuminates her curtains. As my hand goes numb, I do my best to inhale the smell of her tiny head like I'm trying to trap it in my lungs for the next four decades—because I am.

One particular night during the severe slide period, I joined Annie for talk time. I want to be clear that while there were days—more than I'd like to admit—when I was drinking in the afternoons, it wasn't every day. And if I could help it, I'd try to save the heaviest drinking for after the kids (and even Brett) went to bed.

But that doesn't mean I wouldn't usually start with a little something around dinnertime. So, toward the end of my ride on the bucking bronco of bourbon, I usually had a couple drinks in me by the time we started tucking the kids into bed.

This night was one of those nights. And as I settled in for talk time by taking my place next to Annie, hip-to-hip and cheek-to-cheek, she said something that stunned me: "Daddy, have you been drinking your bourbon again?"

My eyes got big. My young daughter already knew what bourbon smelled like. She already knew that there was such a thing as *my* bourbon. And she was already confronting me about it. The fact that she said it with a giggle made it even worse.

I hadn't even had that much . . . yet.

I knew exactly what she was experiencing. I'd learned about that smell as a young kid too. Back then, I associated it with the love, closeness, and affection of certain family members. Alcohol on the breath meant love on the lips because it meant time with and attention from them.

And I didn't want that for my daughter.

I'd like to say that instantly jolted me awake. That I ran downstairs and poured out all my alcohol like I was in some cliché Hallmark movie. But the truth is, I put the feeling on ice with a splash of bitters, a twisted orange peel, and a fistful—not a finger—of bourbon.

That story, though, raises two very important questions about my time spent in the depths of my disorder:

1. *How* was I able to live like that? Me, the Christian. Me, the mental health writer. Me, who spent time on staff at my church. Me, the church-going, Bible-believing, Christ-loving family man. How was *I* able to sit through sermons, serve at church, write a popular Christian book, and even give talks while protecting a secret addiction to alcohol that even my daughter was starting to notice?
2. *Why* was I doing that? What was driving me to do something so counter to what I believed in?

I'm not offended by those questions because they're the questions you should be asking. And they're the questions I should be answering. The answers, though, are not *easy* answers. And the answers have layers—four of them, to be exact: the physical layer, the cultural layer, the mental layer, and the spiritual layer.

Understanding these layers and the need to address each one led me to sobriety and recovery. And as I explain each one, chances are you'll find something you can relate to as well. But one important caveat: Please do not confuse my explaining the how and the why as an excuse for my actions. I get it, that's a fine line. But I'm not looking for a free pass. As we'll talk about in chapter 7, true confession and repentance are still necessary.

The Physical Layer

The physical layer may be the easiest to understand. There's science involved. For example, alcohol use disorder affects the brain.[1] There are also genetic predispositions.[2] Addiction, not surprisingly, runs in my family: I have a loved one who is a recovering gambling addict, my sister—who was killed in a car accident—was addicted to opioids, and my family tree includes several branches with AUD.

In other words, the virus of addiction has survived for generations in the jungles of my bloodline. And instead of lying dormant in me, it awakened at deer camp and then slowly began spreading throughout my body.*

Early in my drinking journey, I was able to somewhat control the sickness. I think that's for a few reasons. First, I hadn't gotten used to crossing my Rubicons. Believe it or not, testing your boundaries takes practice. You dip a toe before you start swimming. Also, I wanted to keep hidden from Brett the darkest parts of myself.

Second, there were practical factors, like being broke in those early years. You can't spend what you don't have.

And third, for many, alcohol use disorder is a progressive disease. It's like a waterfall: The more and longer it flows—even if it starts as a trickle—the greater its ability to cut through rock. By 2023, the stone had cracked. The dam had broken. The river was raging. By then, the physical draw had become a major factor, and I always wanted more. I craved more. I needed more. To say I'm jealous of people who can "just have one" is an understatement.

---

*Remember, this is both a physical *and* a spiritual issue. In fact, I'll talk about epigenetics later, which I believe explains a physical manifestation of a spiritual truth.

Today, I can't. I want more because my body just wants more. I want more because of what it does to me physically. And that's what I mean by the physical disease aspect.

The Cultural Layer

Imagine that what I'm about to say is being delivered in calming, hushed tones as we sit side-by-side, my hand placed on your shoulder: "Have you seen what you're up against in society today?"

Friend, the odds are stacked against you when it comes to alcohol. Our culture doesn't just tolerate alcohol, it promotes it. It doesn't just accept drunkenness, it celebrates it. It doesn't just invite imbibing, it implies it. Alcohol companies spent over $84 million for ads during the 2023 Super Bowl alone.[3] Maybe it's no wonder that Celeste Yvonne wrote an entire book on the perils of "mommy wine culture" that same year, which she explains as "the pervasive message that alcohol helps mothers survive motherhood."[4]

"Alcohol is sold to us as this thing that once we turn twenty-one, we're supposed to incorporate it into our lives," author Holly Whitaker—whose book *Quit Like a Woman* became a *New York Times* bestseller—explains.[5]

You're being bombarded with booze. A worship of whiskey. A wonder for wine. A bow-down to beer. A lust for liquor. "Alcohol is the only drug on earth you have to justify *not* taking," sobriety advocate and author Annie Grace reminds us.[6] We are a society that is obsessed with it. No thing or place is off limits. And that includes our churches.

That may come as a shock to some, but it's true. For me, I was raised in Wisconsin, where there was a beer trailer at every Catholic church picnic. But mixing beer with the Good Book isn't just a Catholic thing. Consider this: A friend recently sent me a picture from a wedding where the *evangelical* officiant started the ceremony with a beer toast at the couple's request.

That attitude toward alcohol among mainline protestants really started brewing—pun intended—around 2010 due to the growing "Christian liberty" movement, led by an influential subculture called the "Young, Restless, and Reformed."[7] Many younger and younger-ish evangelical Christians started reacting against their strict upbringings, which condemned drinking of any kind. In response, they threw themselves headlong into a culture of "beer and Bible."

Sure, there was a recognition that getting drunk was bad. However, since the Bible doesn't *forbid* drinking, it should be enjoyed, not demonized. And honestly, that's true. But rarely were the caveats and cautions emphasized as much as the liberties. That attitude began to spread like wildfire, with surveys conducted around the time showing a shift in evangelical drinking thinking.[8] It became so prevalent, it even led to a stunning rebuke from a prominent leader in the Reformed evangelical movement.[9]

But while others may have used their "Christian liberty" wisely, I didn't know how to handle it. Or, more specifically, my dark heart only wanted to use it as an excuse to chase what my dark heart wanted: easy escape.

I started saying things like:

- "What's the *true* definition of getting drunk anyway?"
- "What's the line between buzzed and drunk? It's not having a .08 blood-alcohol level. That's an arbitrary number!"
- "They didn't have Breathalyzers back in Jesus's day!"*

And while I am responsible for my actions, I can't deny that I used the shifting attitude toward drinking in the evangelical church as a justification. My friend Ericka Andersen—herself a Christian in alcohol recovery—notes how this shift has had a particularly devastating effect on women.

---

* Ironically, I bought one to start testing myself, but it was so cheap it didn't really work.

"More Christians were shunning the hard boundaries of teetotaling fundamentalism, preferring not to be labeled 'legalistic,'" she writes. "This . . . meant church ladies and stay-at-home moms joined the ranks of those tipping back far more frequently than ever before. *It's your right to indulge*, they were told."[10]

But gin and juice in the name of Jesus isn't just for one side of the religious spectrum.

Erin Jean Warde is an ordained Episcopalian priest. In her book about her own sobriety journey, *Sober Spirituality*, she writes, "I can't bring to mind one specific comment—because there are so many—in which progressive Christians make jokes about how they're 'not like those fundamentalists' by somehow illustrating how much they drink or that they drink at church."[11]

The conservative Christians are embracing the drinking "freedom" of the liberal ones, while the liberal ones are drinking to prove they're not as uptight as the conservative ones. And the only point that's being made is that AUD doesn't care how liberal or conservative your theology is. Neither does the devil, as long as he has you trapped.

The Mental Layer

The third layer is the mental one. By "mental" here, I mean two things. First, there's the mental health aspect. That includes my past trauma, which I'll talk about more in the next chapter. But know this: Trauma created wounded and scared parts of me (called "exiles") that had never healed.* I think a lot of us have these wounds that turn into exiled parts of us. Many times they develop early on in life (although not always). And when left unhealed, the wounds create chaos.

---

* The term *exiles* comes from a type of therapy called Internal Family Systems. I'll talk about that more coming up.

Couple those woundings with my clinical anxiety and OCD (which are no doubt connected in some—or even many—ways to the woundings), and I became someone who yearned for ways to escape what I was feeling, to turn my mind off in an effort to find a sliver of relief—especially when something would awaken (or trigger) a wounded exile. And while one of the most destructive ways to find relief is to use alcohol, it's also one of the quickest and easiest. Wide, broad, and easy is the road that leads to destruction, after all (Matt. 7:13–14). And none of that got better as I got older and it went untreated—it only got worse.

Let me be clear, though: Before my major slide in 2021, I had done a lot of work on my mental health. Good work. Helpful work. However, once the massive amounts of stress, anxiety, and depression converged, it showed that I hadn't done *enough* healing and *enough* work on *all* the parts of me. I had dug as deep as I thought I needed to dig at the time to get to the root of the problem. What I didn't realize was that there were even deeper issues, deeper roots. And they were even more sinister.

But that's just one part of the mental layer. There's another part that's just as important. Interestingly, I think it overlaps with the spiritual. It's called cognitive dissonance, and it's one of the most important ideas to understand when it comes to Christians with messy sanctification stories.

Cognitive dissonance is believing one thing and doing another and the uncomfortable feelings that arise from that. It is, by definition, the reason we can know what to do—and even want to do it—and yet choose to do something else. It's also why we can want to *abstain* from something we hate and still partake in it.

Paul gives one of the earliest examples of cognitive dissonance in Romans 7:15–20. I mentioned it last chapter, but here's the full context:

> For I do not understand my own actions. For I do not do what I want, but I do the very thing I hate. Now if I do what I do not want, I agree with the law, that it is good. So now it is no longer I who do it, but

sin that dwells within me. For I know that nothing good dwells in me, that is, in my flesh. For I have the desire to do what is right, but not the ability to carry it out. For I do not do the good I want, but the evil I do not want is what I keep on doing. Now if I do what I do not want, it is no longer I who do it, but sin that dwells within me.

That was me. (It still is at times.)

I knew what was right. I knew what was wrong. I knew what being a follower of Jesus meant—and that meant not getting drunk, at minimum. I was even experiencing conviction, and yet my behavior didn't reflect that. In fact, I learned how to stifle my convictions, and I became *really* good at it. That's all because of cognitive dissonance. Dr. Alison Cook explains what happens when cognitive dissonance runs rampant:

> If you don't consciously face the discomfort of dissonance, you open the door for your mind to start playing tricks on you. . . . You might start to rationalize, defend, or justify the incongruence. . . . Your mind can also start creating elaborate justifications that keep you trapped in unhealthy situations. . . . You start creating a storyline that justifies the discrepancy between what you know to be true and your behaviors that don't quite match up to the truth.[12]

"Elaborate justifications." Sound familiar? I had two I would use a lot. The first looked like using growth in one area to cover weakness in another. For example, at one point I came clean to Brett about a porn addiction. That was a big move. However, I then used the act of coming clean to assuage my conscience and protect my other sacred cow: drinking.

I'd tell myself, *I'm growing. I'm maturing. I'm killing sin, even. And I'm being open about some of my drinking, so that means I'm not fully hiding it. I'm good, right? Right? Right!**

---

* I wasn't necessarily being intentionally manipulative. But in looking back I can see how I was willing to sacrifice certain sins in order to hold on to the one I loved the most.

To be fair, I *was* growing in many ways. The Holy Spirit *was* convicting me. I *was* experiencing genuine transformation and repentance in some areas of my life. In fact, I even donated a kidney to a stranger because God told me to. That's the sanctification process. And in that process, we can undergo refinement in one area before we experience it in another.

"It greatly helps all of us to know that God typically works on *something* specific, not everything at once," prominent Christian counselor David Powlison writes about sanctification.[13] And yet, my sinful nature used that as a way to excuse and cover my misordered/disordered relationship with alcohol.

The second justification I used was *not drinking*. Yup, not drinking.

The truth is that there were several times when I gave up alcohol. The first time was around 2016, when I went to Brett and told her that the Holy Spirit had been convicting me and I needed to take a break. She cried and told me she had been praying for that.*

I can't remember how long the break lasted, but it lasted long enough for me to feel like I had control again. Long enough to assuage my conscience. And long enough to give me an excuse to start drinking again. There were several starts and stops like that, but each time I would pick up right where I left off.

But here's what's important: Every single time I stopped or let up—whether for a day or for a month—I was simply counting the days until I could start again. I didn't quit because I really wanted to. I didn't quit because I fully and completely understood what I was doing to myself and others. I didn't quit because I was genuinely remorseful and repentant.

Sometimes I quit to prove that I didn't have a problem.

Sometimes I quit to pay penance for my actions.

---

* That struck me. I thought I had been hiding everything so well. But if that was the case, why was she praying I would be convicted about my drinking?

Sometimes I quit for my health.

Sometimes I quit because others wanted me to.

But I always quit so I could start again.

Other times, I'd intentionally abstain while out with Brett or friends so I could drink unimpeded and unashamedly when I got home (and give visual breadcrumbs to those around me that I didn't have a problem). I'd also buy goodwill using past moments of restraint. I'd recall, and then find ways to talk about, the rare times when I *was* able to have just a couple and wasn't the drunkest one in the room—like the time I took a trip to New Orleans with some high school friends and returned to the hotel early instead of closing down Bourbon Street. Or that one New Year's Eve back in Wisconsin when I had to help a very drunk friend find his bed, but I was fine. Or the couple weddings I barely drank at.

In the end, even though I wasn't drinking, it was still consuming my mind. And that's still a misordered/disordered relationship with alcohol. That's cognitive dissonance.

The Spiritual Layer

The final layer is the spiritual one. We're partway there when we talk about cognitive dissonance, but there are a few other parts of the spiritual discussion that are important.

The first part is going to sound controversial, but I really don't think it is: We Christians can sometimes get so focused on right teaching and right doctrines that we become inoculated against actual spiritual growth.

In other words, we can be so focused on *believing* all the right things and *saying* all the right things that it can create a barrier to actually *doing* the right things. How? Because we think right ideas make up for wrong actions. And then we stop *experiencing* a relationship with Jesus.

"God did not intend the theology of the Bible to be an end in itself, as if theological knowledge were the goal of grace," author Paul David Tripp reminds us. "No, every part of the Bible's teaching is designed to be a means to an end, and the end is a radically transformed life."[14]

But I fell into that trap. Maybe you have too. And I suspect there are many more out there like us. We get so caught up in having right beliefs and ideas that we ignore the actual beautiful part of cultivating a relationship with our Savior. Don't get me wrong, I *do* believe thoughts, ideas, beliefs, and words are important. But being so caught up in those things at the expense of a relationship can leave us susceptible to the devil's attacks. Why? Because we were created not just to *have* a relationship with Jesus but to *experience* a relationship with Jesus (see John 6:55–59; 15:5; Gal. 4:6).

We get the opportunity to experience a relationship with the living God, and yet many times we settle for playing dress-up. We settle for an imaginary friend instead of a living one. We take the doll over the deity.

I think the best explanation of this concept comes from Heather Kopp, a self-described "Christian drunk" who wrote an incredible memoir called *Sober Mercies*. I relate to Heather on so many levels. Like me, she is a Christian who became an alcoholic while also working within Christian circles. In her book, she talks about her own form of cognitive dissonance:

> Sometimes I acted on [my] beliefs [about God]. More often than not, though, I was pretty sure that just having them—being "right" in what I believed—constituted the greater part of the spiritual life. . . . Working with [my sponsor] Kate, I started to see how *my Christian background had in many ways actually inoculated me against spiritual growth*. For decades, I had heard the same truths over and over in a language that had become so familiar that everything I

heard rang of something I thought I already knew. That meant that for years, deep spiritual truths I heard in church had bounced off of me like a rubber ball off cement. . . . I had mistaken a belief-based faith for an experience-based faith. I'd been on a prideful intellectual journey aimed at being right about God instead of on a desperate soul journey aimed at being real with God.[15]

You want to know how we Christians can fall into such obvious sin sometimes? We get complacent. We sit in church services for decades and trade awe for osmosis. We rely on being right instead of on being in relationship. And when we do that, we become "inoculated against spiritual growth." That's not a dig at our churches and pastors, by the way. It's a reality of sin. It's a reality of human life. We humans fall into complacency very easily. And unless we're taking active steps constantly and consistently to strengthen our spiritual muscles and move toward Jesus, we become lethargic.

This isn't some novel concept, by the way. It's actually been a struggle of Christians for centuries. As Saint Gregory of Nyssa said, "Sin happens whenever we refuse to keep growing."[16]

But we also see it even earlier than that, in the book of Revelation. I get it; that book elicits a lot of controversy, interpretations, and confusion. It's apocalyptic literature that uses a lot of metaphor and imagery, after all. But at its core, the book is a letter to seven different churches. And in chapter 2, Jesus has a special message for the church in Ephesus. That message? In essence, it's that the Ephesian church knows all the right things but has abandoned Jesus.

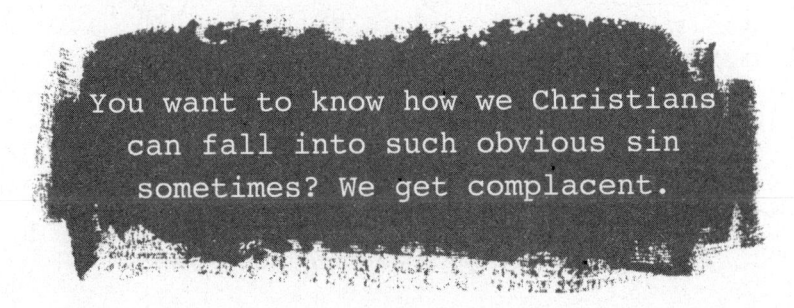

> You want to know how we Christians can fall into such obvious sin sometimes? We get complacent.

"But I have this against you," Jesus says to the Ephesians in verse 4, "that you have abandoned the love you had at first." In his book *The Overcomers*, popular pastor Matt Chandler unpacks this one phrase in very clear terms:

> Despite good doctrine, the ability to spot false teachers, a hatred for evil, and patient endurance, the church at Ephesus had a big problem—their affection and intimacy with Jesus had vanished. Were they committed to orthodoxy? Yes! But their love for Jesus had dwindled. . . . They had good doctrine, but bad devotion.[17]

In other words, they had gotten complacent. They *knew* all the right things, *believed* all the right things, and *said* all the right things—but they missed the mark on implementing them. They didn't have a rich, deep relationship with Jesus. They weren't experiencing him. That was Heather's problem. That was my problem. And I also wonder if it was Adam and Eve's problem too.

See, I think complacency has been a tool of our ultimate enemy since the beginning of time. Think back to the garden of Eden. When did Adam and Eve sin? It's when they were quite literally not walking with God—when they were physically separated from him. They knew the truth, they had been raised on it, so to speak, and even formed by it. And yet, when not physically walking with God, that's when they entertained the devil's lies.

I just don't think that's a coincidence. We can take God, our faith, and our growth for granted. The words of the great preacher Charles Spurgeon ring so true here: "We generally make our worst mistakes in matters which appear to us to be so plain that we think we do not need direction from God concerning them."[18]

Friend, how did I become a Christian alcoholic? Yes, there was a physical layer, a cultural layer, and a mental layer. But there was also a spiritual layer where I fell away from my first love, especially in the year and a half leading up to my rock bottom. I got complacent, and then my affection for alcohol and what it could do for me overtook my love, awe, and affinity for Jesus. And I remember being convicted and ignoring that conviction. I remember making that choice!

That choice affected my relationship with Christ and my closeness with him. Yes, I was following him. But I wasn't walking with him—at least not in the way I needed to be. And in that sense, it's not really hard to understand how I ended up desperate, downtrodden, destitute, and drunk. Very, very drunk.

That's how we Christians can sit through years of sermons, serve as volunteers, and still fall into sin. Dramatic sin. Ugly sin. Obvious sin, even. The church in Ephesus struggled with it. I struggled with it. And chances are—in at least *some* area of your life—you struggle with it too.

Brennan Manning knew this all too well:

> Often I have been asked, "Brennan, how is it possible that you became an alcoholic after you got saved?" It is possible because I got battered and bruised by loneliness and failure; because I got discouraged, uncertain, guilt-ridden, and took my eyes off Jesus. Because the Christ-encounter did not transfigure me into an angel. Because justification by grace through faith means I have been set in right relationship with God, not made the equivalent of a patient etherized on a table.[19]

And that means we Christians—we humans—are a "bundle of paradoxes" who are masters at deceiving ourselves.[20]

We combat that by connecting with God (abiding) in ways that cultivate an experiential relationship with him. I love how Henry Scougal, the great theologian from the 1600s puts it: "True religion is a union of the soul with God. It is a participation in the divine nature. It is the very image of God drawn upon the soul. In the apostle's words, it is Christ formed within us."[21]

Can "True" Christians Fall into Addiction?

I don't want to run away from hard conversations. I think that's clear by now. So I want to confront something head-on. If you're like me, and especially if you start getting vulnerable about your struggle, you may have someone bring up a Scripture passage like 1 John 3:4–10. I won't quote the entire thing, but I'll use two verses to give you the gist. "No one who abides in [God] keeps on sinning; no one who keeps on sinning has either seen him or known him," verse 6 says. And then there's verse 9: "No one born of God makes a practice of sinning, for God's seed abides in him; and he cannot keep on sinning, because he has been born of God." In other words, there are plenty of Christians out there who subscribe to the belief that "true" Christians can't fall into addiction because that would mean they engaged in a prolonged period of sin, and the Bible is *clear* that Christians can't do that.

Well, that's awkward, isn't it?

See, there was a period in my life when I kept on sinning. And sinning. And sinning. In a sense, you could say that I even made a practice out of it. And yet I am 100 percent confident that I was a Christian during that period.

How do I reconcile that?

Fairly easily, actually. First, I think the doctrine of sanctification makes room for it. We'll talk about sanctification more in chapter 7, but remember, it's the idea that we are continually being made more like Jesus from the moment we begin following him. And that is a process. In fact, earlier, in 1 John 2:1 the author acknowledges this process: "I am writing these things to you so that you may not sin. *But if anyone does sin*, we have an advocate with the Father, Jesus Christ the righteous" (emphasis added).

Jesus *himself* talks about this. In the parable of the lost sheep (Matt. 18:12–14), the sheep is actually a *believer* who "wanders away" (v. 12 NIV) and has "gone astray," not an unbeliever.* You can add Paul (Gal. 6:1) and especially James to the list: "We all stumble in many ways" (James 3:2).

But Jon, that's different. You admit that you intentionally kept on getting drunk even when you knew deep down it was wrong!

You're right, I did. And you know what? I eventually stopped. That brings me to my second point. I believe that 1 John 3:6 can just as easily be used to show that I *was* a Christian during my period of misordered/disordered drinking. How? Because I couldn't, and didn't, stay stuck in that sin pattern forever! Eventually, the Holy Spirit's conviction became too heavy. I broke. I stopped. I got free.

So here's my question: How long does a period of ongoing sin have to be before it's considered evidence of no previous salvation? Is it one week? One year? Three years? Twenty years? Also, what kind of sin qualifies as the type that signals you were never really a true Christian? Does gluttony count? Does anger? How about jealousy, pride, or envy? Or is it just the more overt sins like adultery and addiction? And finally, what proves that someone is doing battle against an ongoing sin? Do they have to make it obvious to *everyone*? What about the conflict and torment they're feeling inside?

The point is, different people would answer those questions differently. And that's why *we* don't get to answer them. God does. All we can do is look at the final result. And if someone who has previous evidence of a true, genuine conversion (which I did) falls into a habitual pattern of sin for a period of time—and then is able to break free from that sin this side of glory—I think we have to conclude not that they were never "saved" but that it is precisely because of the ongoing work of the Holy Spirit who came during the person's conversion that they were able to break free.

---

* In Luke's Gospel (15:3–7), Jesus tells a similar story but alters it slightly to make it about unbelievers. In other words, Jesus will chase after you both *before* you follow him *and* after. That's beautiful!

"This is the painful reality," Will Timmins writes. "Our bodily condition hasn't yet caught up with who we now are in Christ."[22]

I have that confidence. And I want you to have that confidence too.

———

I want to be clear that the addiction conversation requires care. There are a lot of things at play when it comes to alcohol use disorder. And so some recovery advocates really bristle at including the word *sin* when talking about AUD—the secular ones, of course, but even some Christian ones. But I just don't think we can get around the fact that drunkenness is a sin, and so is idolatry. There may be layers of reasons we engage in a misordered/disordered relationship with alcohol, but our propensity *to* sin as well as the result *of* sin breaking this world are two of them. And in the end, you could say they are the deepest reasons.

"Calling people 'sinful' is no more judgmental than a doctor telling a patient they have a liver condition," pastor and author John Mark Comer writes. "It's just honest."[23]

I wrote extensively about this in my book on mental health, and I think the same thing applies here: The sinful act is not in having the struggle; it's not in the pull toward alcohol, escapism, idolatry, or drunkenness. The sinful act is what we do with that pull. (Although sin entering the world caused these distorted pulls in the first place.)

I like how Kopp puts it:

> These days, I see myself as an ordinary person with a physical and mental predisposition that will never go away but that no longer defines my life. And I also know I'm a sinner saved by grace—not just once so I can get into heaven, but every day so I can live sober, happy, and free.[24]

That brings me to the last aspect of the spiritual: spiritual warfare.

This is something I've traditionally struggled to fully embrace. I grew up in a faith denomination that overspiritualized nearly everything—including getting the prime parking spot at Walmart. So I've historically wrinkled my nose at the idea of spiritual warfare.

Not anymore.

See, there's still a part of me that can't fully make sense of every detail of the how and why. If you have a misordered/disordered relationship with something, you'll get that. There's a part of this that just, well, is. It's just there, and everything we've talked about so far contributes. How was I able to know the truth and still struggle? Because we live in a fallen world where our bodies crave substances, our minds long for escape, our sinful nature believes lies, and we continue to do what we don't want to do even though we've been redeemed. That's Paul's summary. I mentioned the actual quote earlier, but there's even more that comes after the "I do what I hate" part. In Romans 7:21–25 he gives an important summary:

> So I find it to be a law that when I want to do right, evil lies close at hand. For I delight in the law of God, in my inner being, but I see in my members another law waging war against the law of my mind and making me captive to the law of sin that dwells in my members. Wretched man that I am! Who will deliver me from this body of death? Thanks be to God through Jesus Christ our Lord! So then, I myself serve the law of God with my mind, but with my flesh I serve the law of sin.

Paul, the great Christian, admits that "when I want to do right, evil lies close at hand" and "with my flesh I serve the law of sin." The only hope for such a "wretched man"? Jesus.*

You know what all that's called? That's spiritual warfare. It's where the worldly and the otherworldly collide. And it's real.

---

* Paul repeats this idea in 1 Timothy 1:15: "Christ Jesus came into the world to save sinners, of whom I am the foremost." Every major Bible translation renders the Greek verb (*eimi*) there as "am," not "was."

There are "cosmic powers" and "spiritual forces of evil in the heavenly places" (Eph. 6:12). The devil is at work. My favorite author, C. S. Lewis, sums this up well in his masterpiece *The Screwtape Letters*. And I like how Alison Cook quotes him:

> The father of lies is the master con artist. He's dulled our senses and duped our minds with cheap naming counterfeits. He knows the power of a mental haze "to steal away [your] best years not in sweet sins but in a dreary flickering of the mind over it knows not what and knows not why."[25]

Some of my best years were spent in a mental haze and a "dreary flickering of the mind" that I couldn't fully make sense of. Why? One of the big reasons is spiritual warfare. I have an enemy. He wants me dead. He wants me inoculated against spiritual things. He wants me incapacitated and ineffective. And like a good enemy, he knows and exploits my weaknesses. He wants to "devour" me (1 Pet. 5:8). I know that now. I'm not ignoring it. And in some ways, if I'm honest, I now wear that as a badge of honor.

I didn't always. For so long I struggled with being the "Christian mental health guy" who then fell for alcohol like it was a teen heartthrob. Now? I like to think that the work I was doing was so important, so powerful, that my enemy had to focus so much energy on dulling my effectiveness.

Maybe that's part of why you find yourself where you're at. Your past relationship with Jesus, your future relationship with Jesus, is so scary to our enemy that he's throwing everything he has at you. And the crack that alcohol has caused in your armor may be his best way to make sure you don't, or can't, pick up your sword.*

---

* *But Jon, I'm actually pretty effective right now*, you might say. I thought I was too. And that should scare you even more. Because imagine what you *could* be doing if you didn't have this whole alcohol thing holding you back.

The last thing I'll say on all these layers is that your story may be different. Maybe you don't quite have the physical draw toward alcohol that I had (and have). Or maybe you're more of an amateur when it comes to the mental gymnastics and not Simone Biles like I was. Maybe your story sounds more like how Chandler describes it:

> In the past few years, many of us have fallen out of the rhythms that make us so dreadful to the enemy. We needed to retreat into our homes and attempt to be good neighbors despite the consistently inconsistent information around the pandemic. We couldn't gather with other believers in person, and new coping mechanisms became the norm for many of us. Our old compulsions or new ones flared. Where we thought we had victory over pornography, it reared its head again; that one glass of wine became three; we began to comfort ourselves with food; our screen time went up 900 percent a week; and our consumption of Netflix and Amazon Prime probably doubled. We're out of fighting shape and, if we're honest with ourselves, a little ashamed, or maybe we have simply grown comfortable on the sideline.[26]

Remember, this is all a spectrum. Maybe you're not quite as far to the right as I was. Instead of using that as an excuse to keep going, I'd encourage you to use this as a sign to take an exit. This is your opportunity to turn around. Don't let it get to the point that I let it get to.

You have the clues to how this can happen. Now please, use them to your benefit.

FIVE

Root vs. Fruit

> We will continue to live out of our childhood wounds if we don't stop to acknowledge the wounds, heal the wounds, and break the patterns of pain.
>
> —Debra Fileta

The temperature is frigid.

I'm not old enough to know what "below freezing" is, but it's well below that. It's the middle of the Wisconsin winter, after all, and I'm outside with only a diaper on.

I'm yelling, but my voice is weak—and getting weaker. I'm knocking on the door, but because of my age—which is somewhere in the early toddler stage—it's more of a tap. And with each passing minute, it's becoming fainter.

I'm shaking, both from the cold and from the fear. I'm too young to know what death is, but I'm old enough to feel the helplessness and dread that accompany it looming over me. Watching me. Waiting for me.

And then . . .

After what seems like forever, I see the door open. My mom, beside herself, scoops me up. She puts me in a blanket and sits next to the fireplace and rubs me all over. I'm safe. It's over. I'm OK.

That is one of my recurring nightmares. It's based on a story I was told growing up about how I once locked myself out of the house amid the chaos of bringing in the groceries. And it has always haunted me. In the formative years of my life, that dream gave way to a core belief—a core lie—that has guided so many unhealthy decisions: *You have been and will be forgotten; you have been and will be abandoned. No one cares about you.*

That lie is part of my "root" issues. I told you that at the heart of my drinking is the addiction not just to alcohol but to escapism. But what, exactly, am I trying to escape *from*? That's the question that came into focus the day on the beach with Brett when she told me I had to get to the bottom of why I drank. The drinking was just the fruit of something that went deeper.

Much deeper.

"If you are trying to deal with an addiction, simply by stopping that specific problematic behavior, you're not actually dealing with the addiction," licensed Christian counselor and author Debra Fileta explains. "It will eventually come back or take a different form. Dealing with the addiction means getting to the roots of where it's coming from and why you do it. Real and lasting healing only happens when you deal with what's going on inside."[1]

It wasn't enough to just stop drinking. Even if I never let alcohol tickle my taste buds again, the escapism would manifest in some other way. Eventually. It always did. It had been porn; now it was alcohol. Who knew what else was waiting to whisk me away to Numbing Numbingland?

This idea is encapsulated in the scientific study of epigenetics. I had never heard that term until I started digging into my past. But once I did, so much made sense.

Epigenetics, as the Harvard Center on the Developing Child explains it, studies how "adverse fetal and early childhood experiences can—and do—lead to physical and chemical changes in the brain that can last a lifetime."[2] Simply put, early childhood trauma can very literally change our bodies and our minds and even how our genes are expressed.*

I love how addiction recovery advocate—and now addiction recovery mentor of mine—Caroline Beidler explains it: "The things that happen to us and to our families are a part of us, a part of our genetic make-up, and breathe death into our very lives today."[3]

I've had people ask me, "What does a rough childhood have to do with your drinking?" On a scientific level, epigenetics is the answer.†

Intuitively, I knew this. I knew there were things from my childhood that were driving my escapism. But that's about it. That's why I chose a therapist who specialized in EMDR trauma therapy. I needed her to guide me. To help me see the lurking monsters that I had never fully faced. It was time to take a voyage into the darkest parts of myself and slay whatever minions were there. These were uncharted waters. I didn't have all the weapons. But I knew it had to be done. Either I was going to kill them or they were going to kill me—figuratively and maybe even quite literally.

You need to kill those monsters too.

---

* Licensed Christian counselor Gina Birkemeier unpacks in her book *Generations Deep* how epigenetics explains the use of the term *generational curses* in the Bible. Instead of being a pronouncement of judgment, these curses are really just describing epigenetics. I think she's right. In other words, science has caught up to the Bible once again.

† However, everyone's lived experience is different. Some people can go through trauma and not experience the harmful effects. Praise God!

Numbing Instead of Naming

Before I tell you what monsters I found, we need to have a quick discussion on numbing behaviors.

I recently had two root canals in the same year because I grind my teeth at night. When I first started encountering the tooth pain, though, I didn't immediately go to the dentist. No, I bought some numbing gel and began putting it on for relief. As the pain got worse, I had to put more and more gel on until it was an almost constant routine. Finally, after it got so bad I couldn't eat, only *then* did I schedule a dentist appointment, and by that time it was an emergency.

That's what we do with our root issues. We experience the pain they cause, but instead of dealing with them head-on, we take the easier route: We numb them. Unfortunately, those numbing behaviors have side effects. And those side effects can be disastrous. Never mind the fact that the underlying issue continues to grow and fester.

That was me. Remember, drinking wasn't my "problem"; it was the easy (but unhealthy and destructive) solution to my problems. It was my numbing, my coping, mechanism.

Friend, we all numb to a certain extent. And in fact, there are *healthy* ways to do so. We'd be a mess if we constantly dwelled on our deepest, darkest issues. But the problem is, we look for the path of least resistance. Instead of going on a run, for example, I took to drinking. The side effects of running, though, are good and healthy. The side effects of drinking away your emotions are everything but.

A word of caution, though: We can develop a misordered/disordered relationship with *any* numbing or coping mechanism, even the healthy ones. Our hearts are idol factories, after all, as John Calvin said.[4] Plenty of people do that with exercise, for example. You've seen that, right?

We need to heed Dr. Alison Cook's caution:

> Problems arise when otherwise healthy activities become numbing behaviors. You mindlessly eat, binge-watch, scroll, work, dive into someone else's problems, shop, or drink instead of tending to the needs of your heart. You're not naming what's hard and coping with it. You're numbing.[5]

So how do we know when something has become an unhealthy numbing or coping mechanism? Dr. Cook gives us a simple rubric:

> (1) The behavior is disrupting things you need, such as sleep, nutrition, connection with others, or financial stability. (2) The behavior is compulsive; you want to stop but you can't. (3) There's an element of secrecy; you don't want other people to find out what you're doing.[6]

Check. Check. And check. My relationship with alcohol satisfied all three of those components. Does yours? Or maybe if it's not your drinking, does your eating? Does your exercise? Does your gaming? Does your shopping?

If so, I implore you to name it. And then to do the hard (and yes, uncomfortable) work of getting to the bottom of why you're doing it. For two reasons: (1) because like I said earlier, if you don't, you'll just end up trading one cruel master for another; and (2) there's something so much better and more fulfilling waiting for you if you do. That may not seem possible right now, but I'm telling you it's true.

Listen to how Dr. Cook describes the other side of your misordered/disordered relationship:

> When you name, you come alive to yourself and to God and to the wonder all around you. You feel that wild surge of aliveness as you savor the feeling of fresh soil under your feet or lose yourself in the starry sky as night descends. You honor the tears that well up in your eyes as a tender moment overtakes you. You delight in

the laughter that bursts forth as you rehash a child's antics. You marvel at the flash of insight or the epiphany that comes when the dots of a problem you've been wrestling with suddenly connect. You cherish the surprised yet grateful feeling in your heart as you contemplate a loved one's actions. You are transformed by the almost imperceptible voice of God's Spirit whispering, *Your life is precious*.[7]

Oh, how true that was for me. As I've given up my unhealthy numbing behavior and gotten to the root, I'm relearning who Jon is. Or maybe I'm really learning who Jon is for the first time. I even joke that I have more pictures of sunsets, nature, and birds on my phone than someone who isn't retired should have. Who knew I loved clouds so much?

I want that for you (including the sunsets). But more importantly, God wants that for you.

How I Got to the Root

Getting to my root involved a very intentional practice. Every week for nearly a year, I'd drive to a building located in the old town square of the Dallas suburb where we live. I'd park my truck under a live-oak tree, walk past the ballerinas sashaying in the window of the dance studio on the ground floor, and then take the elevator four floors up to my therapist Gina's office.

I'd walk in the door and immediately take a seat in the chair on the left.* Once seated, I would grab the small, yellow, tasseled pillow, perfect for fidgeting while admitting uncomfortable things. Without much prompting, I'd start talking about what I had experienced that week and what I thought about it. Without alcohol, I noticed how many more thoughts I had. How many more emotions. And when we got to a troubling one, we'd stop, we'd

---

* I sat in the right-hand chair *once* and regretted it. I'm team left chair for sure.

pray, and I'd pick up a set of vibrating, egg-shaped apparatuses, one for each hand.

The premise of EMDR therapy is that through bilateral stimulation—engaging both sides of your brain at the same time—you're able to access thoughts, emotions, and memories that your amygdala has locked away to protect you from trauma. Once you reprocess those memories in a safe environment, you're able to overcome unwanted responses to that trauma.*

So I'd close my eyes and Gina would walk me through a series of prompts and exercises to identify my earliest memory of having whatever uncomfortable emotions we identified as the apparatuses vibrated: left, right, left, right, and so on. We'd talk about what I was seeing, what I was feeling (physically and emotionally), and what I believed about myself (both healthy and unhealthy). We'd chase images, scenes, and experiences. And I'd cry.

Then we would invite Jesus in. We'd ask him to replace the lies with truth and to heal the traumas. We'd listen for what he was telling me. We'd talk through what he was saying, or why I was struggling to hear anything at all. And then we'd do it all again the next week. And the week after. And the week after that. Until truth became more prevalent than the lies, until curiosity overtook the shame, and until what was once traumatic to think about was reprocessed healthily, honestly, and completely.

Throughout that year, I was also introduced to the difference between the strong, thriving, healthy parts of me and the wounded, scared, unhealed parts of me ("exiles")—as well as the parts that stepped in to try and protect those wounded parts (called "managers" and "firefighters"). These terms are part of a helpful form of

---

* The best way I can describe this process is that if other forms of therapy help you get over your struggle, EMDR helps you uncover *why* you struggle. But for a more thorough explanation of the science behind EMDR, you can read about it on the EMDR Institute website at https://www.emdr.com/what-is-emdr-therapy-layperson/.

therapy called Internal Family Systems (IFS).* My strong, healthy parts wrote a book and could recite and spout right beliefs while following the Holy Spirit's prompting to root out certain sins. The scared, wounded exile parts of me had been hurt by trauma, were insecure, and believed numerous lies. And when those parts re-emerged, re-awoke, or were re-wounded, the protective firefighter parts stepped in and remembered that the easy way to cope with the resulting uncomfortable emotions, thoughts, and responses—to put out the fire—was to drink them all away. In other words, the protective parts of me would try to soothe the awakened hurt parts of me by turning to the quickest, easiest coping mechanisms. Because, absent new tools and a complete understanding, that's what I had learned to do early on.

In that sense, there was/is a *part* of me that struggles with abusing alcohol and using it sinfully (an "alcoholic") but that part is not *all* of me.† Unsurprisingly, this is biblical. We talked last chapter about Paul's comments in Romans 7 on doing what he doesn't want to do, but he also repeats the idea in Galatians 5:17: "For the desires of the flesh are against the Spirit, and the desires of the Spirit are against the flesh, for these are opposed to each other, *to keep you from doing the things you want to do*" (emphasis added). The Greek word Paul uses for "flesh" there (and in Romans) is *sarx*. It doesn't mean flesh and bones in this context. Instead, it refers to our sin nature, our sinful hearts. Or, as Tim Keller beautifully and importantly explains, "It is the part or the aspect of our hearts which is not yet renewed by the Spirit."[8]

Did you catch that? Your sinful nature is the "part" of you yet to be fully exposed to Jesus and the Spirit. Not all of you, a part. And we all have that part. Those parts, really. As we've seen, Paul

---

* Think of the animated movie *Inside Out* and picture our parts as the different emotional characters in that movie. For a deeper description, see *Boundaries for Your Soul* by Dr. Alison Cook and Kimberly Miller.

† It's quite possible for a part like that to heal only to be re-wounded, or for an exiled part that you never knew existed to be awakened due to some trigger and want the "quick fix" as well.

certainly did. Even James talks about the passions that are at war within (James 4:1–3).

As I came to understand all this, I found there were four main trauma areas the wounded, scared parts of me struggled with (so far). They were my roots, so to speak. And while there are numerous definitions of trauma you could use, I think for our purposes I love what Dr. Dan Siegel says—that we are born with a desire for four things: to be seen, soothed, safe, and secure.[9] Our traumas, then, can be traced back to feeling a lack of one of those four things and not having an "empathetic witness" to help walk us through it at the time, as Gabor Maté, a doctor and renowned trauma expert, says.[10]

My Roots
Root 1: My Personality

I can't tell you the first time I heard it. I'm not even sure the words were meant to cut me like they did. But the truth is, they became some of the most confusing and devastating sentences for my young mind to process.

At a young age, I was repeatedly told how hyper, how energetic, and especially how loud I was by numerous people, including family. Eventually, it morphed into me being *too* hyper, *too* energetic, and especially *too* loud. In fact, I can still see and hear certain people telling me as much. To this day, my voice carries, and every time someone points it out, it still stings.

Somewhere along the way, all the shushing and the attempts to contain and curtail my personality morphed into some destructive beliefs: *I am embarrassing, I am unwanted, I am a burden, and in order to be accepted, I must be something else.*

"These thoughts grew up with me and became my internal operating system, subconsciously shaping my external world," Matt Chandler explains, describing my own life almost perfectly while explaining how similar words spoken to him affected his life. "It took nearly thirty years before I figured out those thoughts were short-circuiting certain areas of my life."[11]

The words spoken *over* us—good and bad—turn into the mantras and beliefs that take root *inside* of us, which then end up *guiding* us. For years, I dealt with those words and especially the beliefs they birthed by drinking them away.*

Root 2: My Childhood

My parents divorced when I was about three years old. For most of my life, I said it never affected me. After all, I have no memories of our family being together.

Then I started my intensive therapy and realized how wrong I was.†

As we started digging, I quickly realized how the feelings and fears of abandonment I've carried with me my entire life started with my parents' divorce. That's certainly because of my dad leaving in the middle of the night with no explanation and not being a significant part of our lives afterward, but also because my mom's focus shifted when she had to become the sole breadwinner—and that created a lot of chaos.

Overnight, my mom became a single mother of four kids. We lost everything, including our "dream home." Understandably, she had to work extra long and extra hard to provide for us, but it was barely enough to make ends meet. So many times we didn't have money for much beyond basic necessities—and even those were

---

* My son—who is a carbon copy of me—is told similar things. And when I hear those words spoken over him, I shudder. During our nightly prayers, then, I make a point to say how thankful I am for his energy, his volume, and his personality and let him hear me ask God to use all of those things for his good and God's glory.

† Let me be clear: The goal of my therapy wasn't to manufacture trauma. I'm sure there are some bad therapists out there, just like there are bad doctors and bad mechanics. But my therapist has never suggested a root cause for my escapism. She's let me explore it with God and come to my own conclusions.

hard to come by. For example, our school sack lunches frequently consisted of whatever my mom could scrounge up—sometimes it was a single bag of microwave popcorn, other times it was liver sausage.* At one point we had to rent the upstairs of a house where my oldest sister's "room" was nothing more than a closet off the family room. And when that landlord wanted to sell, he made us leave immediately instead of letting us stay until we could find something else. The remedy? We packed up and moved into another family's basement.

My mom recently reminded me of some of the other "family traumas" we were forced to endure during this time, all of which created a fifteen-year chaos that hovered over us like a stuck hurricane. And what rained down were doubts, despair, and—eventually—drunkenness.

There was the time my mom came down with a strange disease the doctors couldn't diagnose. Stumped, they tried convincing her to see a psychiatrist because they thought she was making it up. After she lost her vision and couldn't formulate sentences, they finally opened up her skull expecting to find brain cancer. They quickly realized it was bacterial meningitis acquired on a recent mission trip to Guatemala. She was hospitalized for over a month, and each one of us kids lived with different family friends while she was in the hospital. Several times we got calls that we thought would be to say she had died.

While she did survive and eventually regain her vision, it was a long road back to full recovery. She even had her driver's license revoked for a time because of her vision and had to literally walk a mile (and back) in order to get to work.

Then there were the five miscarriages she endured after she married my stepdad. That's an emotional toll that wasn't just felt by

---

* I remember taking one bite of the liver sausage and nearly throwing up. My teacher went around to the other students and solicited leftovers and donations so I'd have something to eat.

her. When she did finally have a long-term pregnancy, my younger brother, Josh, was born three months premature. He weighed one pound, nine ounces and was about the length of a stick of butter. For six months, every night we drove forty-five minutes to a special hospital and spent time with him in the NICU. We frequently got calls in the middle of the night telling us to rush to the hospital because he wasn't going to make it.

By several miracles, he did survive. But when we brought him home, he was on oxygen for two years and had nearly round-the-clock in-home nursing care. Couple that with the fact that we had to turn the living room into his bedroom so he was easily accessible, and even our physical home wasn't a place of peace. Never mind the fact that he was attached to several monitors that would go off at all hours of the day and night. While many times it was simply because something got dislodged, we never knew if the next alarm was "the end."

Even after my younger brother's health improved, the chaos continued. While we had moved into our own home by this point, my parents never forgot what it was like to have so little. That meant we were constantly welcoming the downtrodden and destitute. While it was a kind gesture, it was at the expense of a lot of peace. We had families live with us, we gave a room to an alcoholic, and we even had a nomadic woman take up residence in our basement. I'll never forget walking down to grab some laundry and finding her sleeping on a bed she had made out of an old door. Fearing she was dead, I put my finger just below her nose to see if she was breathing, only to have her open her eyes and give me a look that horror movies are made of. I was maybe ten. After finally asking her to leave, we found her months later living in an old barn on our property.

There were also the several times when the small business my mom owned (and that kept us afloat) faced growing pains. On numerous occasions she had to defer her paycheck or cut her own salary just to pay her employees. That meant *we* went with less instead of someone else.

And then there was the season when my stepdad went into kidney failure. He was so sick and weak that he didn't work for a year while he was on dialysis. Once again, the possibility of losing a loved one was painfully real. Eventually, he did get a kidney transplant, but our emotional and monetary margin was non-existent.

Throughout all this, my mom did the best she could to keep things normal and shield us from the fallout. But not even her Herculean efforts could do that. For instance, I remember being forgotten at church after some services or the school having to call her at work because someone forgot to pick me up. Every single instance like that had an effect on me.*

My point in all this is to say that chaos was a closer companion growing up than peace. As a result, I developed a constant fear of not having enough, of losing someone I loved, of being abandoned or forgotten. I struggled to feel seen, I struggled to feel cared for, and—at times—I struggled to feel safe. Unsurprisingly, I always felt on edge. I was anxious. I was angry.

And the devil loves those feelings.

He's used them to fill my head with lies. Lies like *I don't matter* or *I am inadequate*. He's also used them to drive me toward people-pleasing, toward endless striving, and especially toward escape.† Those feelings would pop up throughout my adult life—sometimes when I didn't have enough money to buy something I wanted or when I was overstimulated or after a comment from a boss. And when they did, it was always easiest to drink them away.

---

* I don't disparage my mom, though. Eventually, because of her tenacity, wisdom, business sense, and hard work, we went from nothing to thriving. She is one of the most amazing women I know and has been recognized as one of Wisconsin's most incredible small-business owners.

† And much to my wife's chagrin, I can also be somewhat of a hoarder at times.

Root 3: My Stepdad

My mom got remarried to my stepdad within a couple years of my parents' divorce. And while my stepdad was one man, I remember him being two very distinct and different people.

The stepdad of my younger years struggled, going from a never-married man with no kids to a father of four overnight. He was prone to fits of anger, and when he got mad, we knew it and especially felt it—the same way his father made him feel it growing up. For example, he had strict rules about obedience and what that had to look like. If we broke those rules, we were spanked. And if we didn't take those spankings the way he thought we should, it led to many more, often while he quoted Scripture.

His annoyance would turn to berating and belittling when he reached a boiling point, sometimes for the smallest things, like not sweeping the kitchen properly. And while I still have positive memories of him during this time, there was a fog of fear, anger, and hurt that hung over our family. That led to feelings of resentment because I wasn't being properly protected.

But then there was the stepdad of my teen years and beyond. That stepdad was one of the calmest and kindest humans I have ever encountered. He was gentle. He was soft. He was a pushover, in fact. My siblings and I would even get frustrated because we knew that he knew people were taking advantage of his generosity, but he didn't care.

That stepdad emerged after some intensive inpatient treatment and therapy for his own issues. My mom stepped in, and he went away to a Christian counseling center in Florida and had a type of road-to-Damascus experience. When he returned, he was truly a changed man. I loved that man. Deeply.*

---

* The irony is not lost on me that, like my stepdad, I have undergone my own midlife transformation as the result of repentance. I understand his struggles better now.

But that didn't erase the traumatic experiences, the fear, the lies, the anger, the resentment, or the trauma responses I developed as a result. No, the devil made sure of that. They'd stay dormant until triggered by situations that made me feel humiliated, embarrassed, rejected, sad, fearful, or stressed. Maybe it was during an argument with Brett or after receiving even the slightest negative feedback or when I outright failed at something. And you know how I dealt with those? The way culture tells us to: *I could really use a drink.*

Root 4: My Sister

I can still hear the screams.

To say my sister, Jenny—who was two years older—made my family's life hell growing up would be an understatement. From a very young age she would fly into fits of rage when she didn't get her way. There was screaming—so much screaming—as well as physical and emotional violence. I've never seen someone actually possessed, but I think it would look like what would happen to Jenny all too frequently.

At one point, my parents sent her away to a Christian girls' home to help her and give us relief. And while it was one of the most peaceful years of my childhood, that peace didn't last long when she returned. The fits of rage were soon made worse by a teen pregnancy and then a drug addiction that would land her in prison. I remember during some of her violent, chaotic, and possessed-like episodes I would sneak onto the roof of our house, cover my ears, and sob as I rocked back and forth, praying it would all stop.

It didn't.

But there was something else with Jenny that complicated things. When I was very young I remember her introducing me to ways my body worked that I had never known before. She would do things of an intimate nature to me and have me do the same to her. Not only did she steal my peace growing up, but she also stole my innocence. And I never knew what to do with that.

Then came 2018. In a twisted turn of events, Jenny was killed in a head-on car crash. Someone else crossed the median, hit her van at over seventy miles per hour, and she died instantly.

Despite our complicated relationship, I was sad. I grieved. And in the immediate aftermath of her death, I was actually quite strong. But those feelings would periodically—and eventually more frequently—give way to confusion and questions I didn't know what to do with:

- *How can I both hate what someone did to me and love them at the same time?*
- *Where did she learn to do what she did to me?*
- *How can I be so mad at her and yet so sad about her death?*
- *How do I reconcile telling her I wished she were gone at times because of what she had done and then grieving when it happened?*
- *And what does that say about me as a Christian?*

My experiences with my sister had lasting effects. For starters, an angry voice of any kind has historically done something to me internally—both physically and emotionally—that's hard to explain. The best way to describe it is that I freeze. See, when we encounter unwelcome or sudden stimuli, we have three main responses: fight, flight, or freeze. In those early years, I gravitated most toward freeze. I shut down.*

That would wreak havoc on my relationships later on. For example, any *slight* elevated or even exasperated tone in Brett's voice would cause a freeze response. That made it hard to have tough, but necessary, conversations for most of our marriage.

---

* This is not to be confused with the actual psychological and physiological phenomenon of shutting down, which is more like dissociation.

In addition, my young son is prone to loud outbursts as he learns to manage his own big emotions. Early on, I struggled with how to connect with him because those outbursts would cause me to either flee or freeze.

Another licensed Christian counselor and author, Aundi Kolber, sums up my predicament: "I tried to explain it, but really how do you explain a feeling that is so visceral you can cut it with a knife? You just feel it, as your nervous system seems to explode; there isn't any rationalizing it."[12]

Peace in any sort of confrontation, then, was nearly always elusive. And when peace is elusive, it's easier to find it in the bottom of a glass.

Before I move on, you may have noticed that I didn't specifically mention my clinical anxiety and OCD as one of my roots even though I mentioned them earlier as being some of the things that led to a misordered/disordered relationship with alcohol. That's because my mental health issues and my trauma are so intertwined it's hard to fully separate them.

In fact, trauma actually rewires our brains. So while I'm genetically predisposed to my mental health issues just like I am my alcohol use disorder, my traumatic experiences contribute as well. They are two sides of the same coin.

The truth is, I drank to not have to deal with any complicated emotions—and those complicated emotions were the result of both trauma and my anxiety and OCD.

Not an Excuse

One caveat is important here: While my trauma roots explain my actions—like my drinking—they do not excuse them. I didn't get

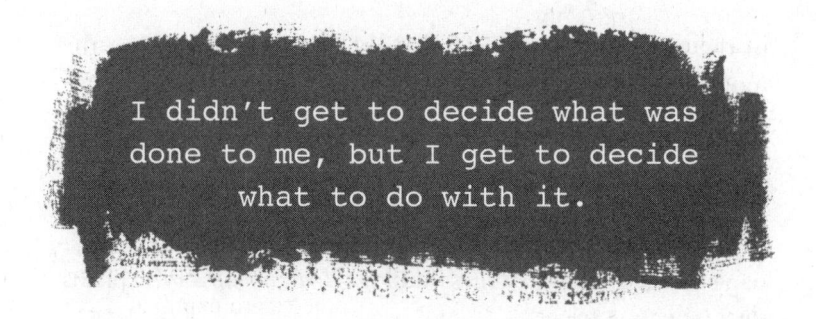

> **I didn't get to decide what was done to me, but I get to decide what to do with it.**

to decide what was done to me, but I get to decide what to do with it.

I get it; that's nuanced. But I don't want to run away from the nuance here.

We see this in the justice system, right? No matter your thoughts on how perfect or imperfect our judicial system is, the truth is that our actions carry weight. The drunk driver can't use as a defense that he was simply drinking away a traumatic experience and shouldn't be held responsible for killing someone in a crash. That would be ridiculous.

I get that's an extreme case, but I think it helps us see the truth: What we do with our trauma is still a choice. If we pursue unhealthy coping and numbing mechanisms, we are responsible for both pursuing those and what happens as a result of pursuing them. We don't get a "get out of jail free" card because we've experienced trauma.

Ultimately, the roots of our traumas go even deeper, to one single thing: Sin has broken and fractured this world. And we can't properly fight sin by engaging in more of it. That's exactly what our ultimate enemy wants us to do. But we can choose something different, something better.

"Too often we clothe ourselves with our trauma to our own destruction," Chandler explains. "I plead with you not to define yourself by that painful experience. I've watched God take some of the worst pain imaginable, heal the person, and redeem the moment by weaponizing it to help others who've suffered similar pain. God can redeem what the enemy used in an attempt to destroy you."[13]

And guess what: God has actually created us with the physical capability to move beyond our trauma. Dr. Lee Warren, a Christian neurosurgeon who writes the blog *Self-Brain Surgery*, explains the fascinating science.

"If you believe that you are stuck with the brain you have because of your . . . past traumas . . . , then I have good news," he writes.[14] That good news, according to Dr. Warren, is called "neuroplasticity," which is the brain's ability to regenerate and make new connections.

"Your brain is literally changing every second of your life. It is structurally different than it was before you started reading this sentence, because of the miracle of neuroplasticity," Warren assures us. In other words, "your brain changes constantly, and you can be in charge of most of those changes."[15]

In that sense you can choose healing. You have that ability. And God created our bodies to respond to it. Enjoy that common grace.

Now What?

So, what do you do with all this? I'm inviting you into my story so that you will be motivated to go on your own journey of curious exploration. That's really the key: curiosity.

Friend, one of the bravest and most courageous things you can do is be curious about the root causes of your misordered/disordered relationship with alcohol or anything else. It's hard. It's not fun. You will feel things you haven't felt in a long time—maybe ever—and don't want to feel. But it is the key to healing, change, and true freedom.

"Don't be alarmed," Dr. Cook says. "Those vulnerable feelings present you with a new opportunity to name, frame, and brave a healthier way to care for yourself."[16]

That's the goal. A healthier way to deal with the brokenness. But it comes through exposing the underlying root of *why* you're actually doing what you're doing first. I'm not necessarily saying that you have unresolved trauma in your life. I'm not saying you were abused as a child. I'm not saying you'll find some of the deep and sinister things that I did. I'm not even saying you have to do EMDR therapy. But if you're reading this book, the truth is, you probably want to stop coping in unhealthy ways and that has proven difficult. The answer? Go exploring. Someway, somehow. Ask Jesus to go on that journey with you. And slay whatever monsters you find.

Today, as a result of getting to my roots, I'm more in tune with myself, I'm more in tune with those around me, but most importantly I'm more in tune with God. Why? Because when you see the ugly parts of yourself and your past, you're forced to recognize that you need God more than ever if you're ever going to be whole and healthy.

I know that may seem elusive, even unattainable. I used to think so too. But I'm telling you it's not. Although I continue to work, dig, and find other roots, I've truly found a peace that surpasses understanding like the Bible talks about in Philippians 4:7. This book is proof of that in my life. And it can be true in your life too.

SIX

Combating Shame

> [God] isn't in love with the future you, the person you might become. He cherishes you right now with all your disappointments and dramas, doubts and fears, anxieties and anger. He sees you, He knows where He's leading you, and He is all-in on His glory being revealed in you.
>
> —Matt Chandler, *The Overcomers*

If there's one word that sums up my feelings while going through the depths of my misordered/disordered relationship with alcohol, it's *shame*.

You don't have to have a story like mine to know exactly what I'm talking about. The truth is, shame is one of the most visceral and universal feelings when it comes to our failures and especially our addictions. In fact, I'm convinced the shame I felt while I was regularly getting drunk despite knowing I shouldn't kept me in bondage a lot longer.

Maybe it's no surprise, then, that shame is one of the devil's greatest tools to keep us trapped in our sins. That's because, instead of drawing closer to Jesus when we feel shame, we run from him like Adam and Eve did in the garden. And the more we run from the light, the easier it becomes to live in the darkness.

Dr. Curt Thompson, who approaches shame from a biblical perspective, writes in his important book *The Soul of Shame* that shame is "the emotional weapon that evil uses to (1) corrupt our relationships with God and each other, and (2) disintegrate any and all gifts of vocational vision and creativity." In fact, it's "a primary means to prevent us from using the gifts we have been given."[1]

Shame separates us from God. It turns us into prisoners. And as prisoners mired in shame we'd rather drink until we can't see our cell before admitting we're trapped in one.

What Is Shame?

OK, so if the devil loves to use shame, what *exactly* is it? That may seem like an unnecessary question. If I asked you to describe shame, you probably could, after all.

But you need to do more than describe something and what it does in order to understand it. You need to define it. And that's where Brené Brown comes in.

You may have heard of Brown before. Her TED Talk on vulnerability and shame is one of the twenty-five most-watched TED videos of all time, with around twenty-five million views. She has been at the forefront of the resurgent conversation around shame, and that's why it's important to make sure you understand how she talks about it. Interestingly, it's a little different than you might think:

> Shame is the fear of disconnection—it's the fear that something we've done or failed to do, an ideal that we've not lived up to, or a goal that we've not accomplished makes us unworthy of

connection. I'm not worthy or good enough for love, belonging, or connection. I'm unlovable. I don't belong.[2]

That fear of disconnection—that unbelonging—plays a bigger role in our lives than we realize, especially as Christians.

It did in mine. My shame told me that if I were found out, I wouldn't be accepted by my wife, I wouldn't be accepted by the church, I would be punished and ostracized, and there was no place in the faith for a hypocrite like me. In other words, it told me I would be cut off from who and what I loved most.

So I hid.

It's been that way since the beginning of humanity's time on earth. In Genesis 3, Adam and Eve usher sin into the world by eating from the tree God told them not to. Instead of admitting their mistake immediately, though, they try to hide it. They try to hide themselves. And they are gripped by fear.

What are they afraid of? I think in some ways they're afraid of the lost connection with God, the trust they just betrayed. They're scared about how they will be seen emotionally, spiritually, and physically. In fact, that feeling becomes so visceral, they even make makeshift clothes out of plants to cover their bodies.*

Friend, that's what shame does to us. We are so afraid of our lost connection that we try to cover it up. And that fear—that shame—forces us into hiding, where the very thing we're ashamed of festers, breeds, and grows.

That's exactly what Brown is talking about. She adds the word "unworthy," and I think that's important. I grew up believing God was a cause-and-effect God. That I had to do certain things to get him to do what I wanted, and that the inverse was also true: If I *didn't* do what he wanted me to, he would see me as unworthy

---

* I think this is more important than we realize. It's a very early and very real example of how what is happening internally manifests externally.

and punish me. Remember, the images I had of a father growing up were either a man who leaves when it gets tough or one who punishes you when you've done wrong.

So when I couldn't stop—or wouldn't stop—drinking, I felt unworthy. And as you probably know all too well, one of the easiest ways to deal with unworthiness is to numb it.

So that's what I did.

When it comes to that shame, it's an especially enticing trap for Christians. Why? Because in some ways we know we are born flawed sinners. We know "no one does good, not even one" (Rom. 3:10–12; see also Ps. 14:1–3; 53:1–3). In that very important sense, we *are* bad. But that's not the bad I'm talking about here. That's a healthy view of our sin nature. Shame, though, takes what's healthy and distorts it. The "bad" our shame feeds off of is more akin to worthlessness. We don't see our value. We sin, and then we let that define us. That's not a proper understanding of the total depravity John Calvin made popular. No, worthlessness is what the devil wants us to feel and to act on.

"Our great enemy wants you stuck in a very real spiritual paralysis because you happen to be an imperfect human," Chandler writes.[3] Like paralysis, shame makes you feel stuck. And that stuck feeling brings me to the shame cycle.

The Shame Cycle

"He just sits in shame and doesn't do anything about it," a friend told me. She was describing her husband, from whom she'd recently separated. He'd been caught in a shame cycle for years, but no matter what she did, she couldn't help pull him out of it.

Making Sense of It

I know all too well what she was talking about. You probably do too.

The shame cycle is that downward spiral we get in that keeps us drinking (or doing whatever else) in order to get over the emotions we have about our drinking (or other destructive actions). And until we deliberately interrupt it, it just keeps going. No one can do it for us.

When it comes to addiction, there are numerous representations of the cycle. None of them are wrong, but I think the one I've outlined below is most specific to our purposes. My shame cycle involves six stages:

1. Drinking
2. Engaging in an unwanted or undesirable behavior
3. Negative self-talk
4. Shame
5. The "Why not?"
6. And finally, more drinking

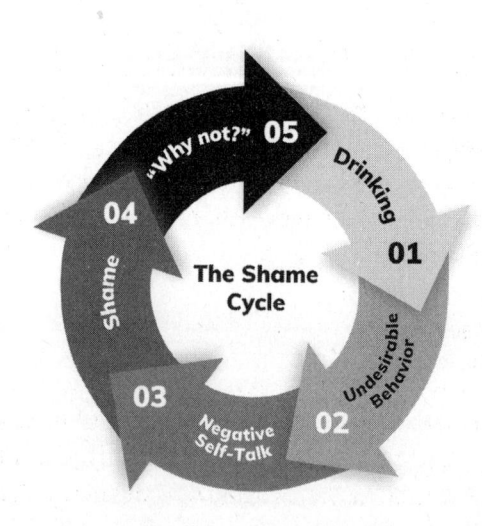

The Shame Cycle

01 Drinking
02 Undesirable Behavior
03 Negative Self-Talk
04 Shame
05 "Why not?"

Stage 1: Drinking

We enter the cycle when we drink. This doesn't mean that every drinking session will end badly. We have a chance to pull the rip cord, so to speak, at a healthy amount. But when you have a misordered/disordered relationship with alcohol, and the further you go to the right on the alcohol use disorder spectrum, the harder it gets to stop at a healthy amount.

Stage 2: Unwanted or Undesirable Behavior

The second stage is where an adverse event happens. Maybe this is where we get drunk. Maybe it's where we go somewhere we shouldn't, do something we shouldn't, see someone we shouldn't. It doesn't necessarily have to mean getting drunk, although it usually does. The key here is that we take an action that then leads to the next stage.

Stage 3: Negative Self-Talk

In stage 3, we realize what we've done, and we become our own worst critic. We start yelling at ourselves, berating ourselves, belittling ourselves. We become our own emotional and verbal abuser—and oftentimes we say things much worse and much more vile than anyone else could ever say to us. "The language of unhealthy guilt is harsh. It is demanding, abusing, criticizing, rejecting, accusing, blaming, condemning, reproaching, and scolding," Brennan Manning explains.[4]

Stage 4: Shame

After listening to ourselves, we then go from "I have done something bad" to "I am bad."[5] In other words, we internalize the negative self-talk to the point that it becomes who we are. As Brown says, we deem ourselves dirty, vile, and unworthy. We then withdraw. Like Adam and Eve, we hide.

Stage 5: The "Why Not?"

This stage is that feeling of being so overwhelmed, so frustrated, so overrun that we don't think it's worth fighting anymore. It's giving up and giving in. The shame is so heavy, and we feel so entrenched and stuck, we say to ourselves, *Well, I've already messed up and gone this far, why not just keep going? Why not just go all in? Why not just really go for it?*

You've been there, right? Poker players call it being "pot committed": You've already bet so much that even though you know you should fold and stop betting, you keep going because you're already too deep. *Why not?*

I can't tell you how many times I did that.

Stage 6: More Drinking

So, what do you do when you decide to go all in? You drink some more. Usually a lot more, because now you're not only trying to numb your root issues, you're also dealing with the shame of going down this path yet again. Like a pregnant mother eating for two, you start ordering everything off the menu because you're drinking for two.

Conversely, this stage can sometimes mean something even more disastrous than more drinking. This is where, when the shame becomes too great, some people take their own lives.

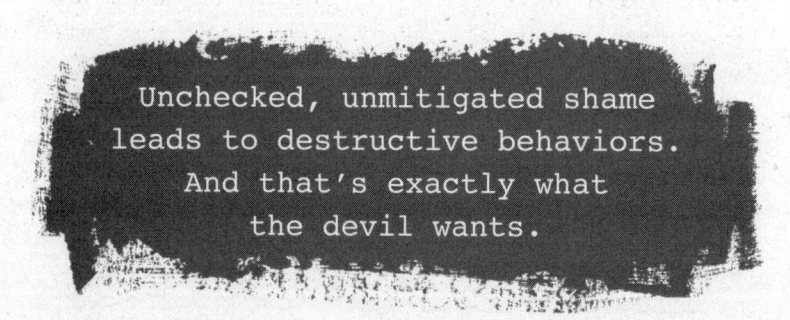

> Unchecked, unmitigated shame leads to destructive behaviors. And that's exactly what the devil wants.

"When we're hurting, either full of shame or even just feeling the fear of shame, we are more likely to engage in self-destructive behaviors and to attack or shame others," Brown explains.[6]

Unchecked, unmitigated shame leads to destructive behaviors. And that's exactly what the devil wants.

Combating Shame

In my initial outline of this book, I titled this chapter "Overcoming Shame." But after really spending time in the research, I'm not sure shame is something we can ever completely overcome. That may sound shocking, but I actually think it's good theology.

Yes, it's true that we *shouldn't* feel shame—just like we *shouldn't* sin. But we live in a fallen world. What I mean is, despite our best efforts, we're *going* to feel shame.

Yes, Jesus overcame shame. God, through the sacrifice of Jesus, covers our shame just like he did in the garden. And when we are with him and this world is fully made new, we won't experience it. But the day of a shame-free world is not today. This side of glory, we will always fight feelings of shame. That's due to our enemy, and in some ways, I think it's also because we know that sin separated us, and continues to separate us, from God. And it will always be a struggle to feel the weight of that in the most healthy way.

So we need to combat it. That's the goal. To create shame resilience, which Brown calls "the ability to practice authenticity when we experience shame, to move through the experience without sacrificing our values, and to come out on the other side of the shame experience with more courage, compassion, and connection than we had going into it."[7]

So, what creates shame resilience? What tool has God given us to fight back? One word: *vulnerability*.

In order to combat our shame we need to *talk* about what we are ashamed of. We need to drag it into the light. We need to expose it. We need to be radically vulnerable. See, there's something pretty incredible that happens when we open up: The light shining through chases away the darkness, and shame loses its power.*

"Healing shame requires our being vulnerable with other people in embodied actions. There is no other way," Thompson sums up nicely.[8]

The irony is that you're more OK when you're talking about how you're not OK than when you're pretending to be OK.

The responsibility to combat shame doesn't just lie with us, though. It's actually a church-wide responsibility. And the prescription is very similar: The church needs to encourage conversations about, and actions of, vulnerability. It needs to have active discussions about embracing Christians with addictions, it needs to facilitate conversations about ongoing sanctification, and it needs to bill itself as the place that welcomes sinners—not just sinners who are finding Jesus for the first time but sinners who already know him and follow him.

Unfortunately, that makes many Christians uncomfortable. And so, is it any wonder that addicts and strugglers find more love and acceptance in the basement of the church, where the twelve-step meeting takes place, than in the sanctuary? In the basement they can bare their souls; in the sanctuary they're expected to not make others feel uncomfortable.

And so much of that is perpetuated not by what's said but by what is *not* said. It's the silence. It's the assumptions of progress. It's the lack of affirmation. It's sermons about Marvel movies instead of God's marvelous grace.

---

* We'll cover vulnerability in depth in chapter 11.

Consider this: A fellow Christian in recovery told me recently that he heard plenty of "attaboys" from those around him when he announced his sobriety, but fast-forward to his one-year sobriety date—a big accomplishment—and he only received one text or call of encouragement. And do you know who it was from? Another former alcoholic in recovery, whom he had never even talked to personally about his sobriety. Nothing from close friends. Nothing from family members, except his wife. Nothing from anyone at his church.

The silence was deafening. And in some ways, that's one of the biggest problems in the church right now. It's the silence.

"Nobody asked me how I was doing," another fellow Christian alcoholic told me when recalling his church experience after entering into recovery. Maybe it's no wonder he relapsed after a long period of sobriety.

I've talked to several others like him—Christians who struggle with a misordered/disordered relationship with alcohol, who were shunned, shamed, ostracized, punished disproportionately, or initially embraced only to be ignored later. And while my personal experience has generally been positive, my fear is that I'm the exception and not the rule.

I get it. The messy sanctification situations are difficult. They take time, patience, care, and wisdom. They love the gray areas. So it's easier to ignore the mess and the person responsible for it.

But please don't take the easy way.

The Bible calls us to associate with sinners, to press into the mess and the messy. Paul even called Peter a hypocrite for not doing so (see Gal. 2:11–14). But I think sometimes we have an easier time drawing close to the unsaved sinner than we do the saved one in our midst. Yet both need attention.

The gospel isn't just for our former lives, our former sins. It's for our current and future ones too. We need to stop talking as if coming to Jesus is all that matters when becoming like Jesus is our ultimate purpose.

If you're reading this and you're a church leader, I want to encourage you to do an inventory of how often you're talking about shame, addiction, grace, forgiveness, and sanctification. I especially want you to do an inventory of how often you're checking in on those you know have struggled or are struggling. I think too many times the church gets stuck in crisis mode: We're quick and good at triage in the emergency room, but then we forget about the patients on the upper floors who need long-term care.

Remember, shame is disconnection. You, church leader or even church attendee, can help break the shame cycle by drawing toward people like me, not away.

Shame vs. Godly Guilt

What, then, should we feel instead of shame? Certainly we're supposed to feel *something* when we've done wrong, right? The answer is *godly guilt*.* Not worldly guilt, but godly guilt. There's a difference and it's important.

For so long, I felt shame but not godly guilt. I don't think I even fully understood what *godly guilt* meant and what it means to feel it. But I want you to. And to do that, we need to start by looking at where godly guilt is unpacked in the Bible.

I think our best explanation of godly guilt comes from 2 Corinthians 7:8–12. Let me set the stage. In the passage, Paul is referencing how he had to call out the Corinthian church. He was slightly apprehensive to do so because he was afraid of their reaction. In the passage, he's responding to *their* response to his previous correction. Here's what he says (and he uses the term *godly grief*):

---

* Some use the term *godly grief* or *godly regret*, but they are all interchangeable.

> For even if I made you grieve with my letter, I do not regret it—though I did regret it, for I see that that letter grieved you, though only for a while. As it is, *I rejoice, not because you were grieved, but because you were grieved into repenting. For you felt a godly grief*, so that you suffered no loss through us.
>
> *For godly grief produces a repentance that leads to salvation without regret, whereas worldly grief produces death.* For see what earnestness this godly grief has produced in you, but also what *eagerness* to clear yourselves, what indignation, what fear, what *longing*, what *zeal*, what punishment! At every point you have proved yourselves innocent in the matter. So although I wrote to you, it was not for the sake of the one who did the wrong, nor for the sake of the one who suffered the wrong, but in order that your earnestness for us might be revealed to you in the sight of God. (emphasis added)

Do you see the effects of godly guilt? Godly guilt produces things like repentance, eagerness, longing, and zeal. Contrast that with shame, which produces isolation, continued misordered/disordered actions, depression, anxiety, loathing, and abusive self-talk. I think pastor John Piper explains the difference well when he says that "the test of whether our grief is of God or of the world is whether it produces change."[9]

In other words, worldly guilt is about you. It's about being embarrassed. It's about wallowing and navel-gazing. It's not about really being sorry for what you've done, but it's about being sorry for getting caught. And it leads to isolation and shame.

Godly guilt, on the other hand, is humble. It's accepting. It isn't defensive. It's understanding the pain and hurt that your sin has caused and looking to take action toward restoration. In fact, while you may be grieved by the sin, there's even a certain "zeal" to undertaking reconciliation.

I'll be honest, I finally felt that toward the end of my drinking. When I sent the email to my therapist on the beach in Miami after hitting rock bottom, it was *finally* out of godly guilt, godly grief, and godly regret. That's why it felt like a weight was lifted off. I was scared, sure, but I was excited to *finally* confront my drinking and especially the underlying issues that were leading me toward a misordered/disordered relationship with alcohol. I had hope.

"A person who has *godly* regret grieves over the terrible thing he has done and believes that only God can help him. God is his only hope," Desiring God cofounder John Bloom explains. "So he turns toward God in faith, confesses his sin, and looks to the cross where the penalty of that sin was placed on the Son of God."[10]

Or, as Manning puts it, "Healthy guilt is one which acknowledges the wrong done and feels remorse, but then is free to embrace the forgiveness that has been offered."[11]

That was me. Finally. And it can be you too.

Judas vs. Peter

However, if you're still struggling with the difference between godly guilt and worldly guilt (aka shame), let me give you a practical example.

On the night Jesus was betrayed, we see two stories of guilt: Judas's and Peter's. Judas betrays Jesus and is so torn up, he takes his own life. Peter betrays Jesus (through his denial of him) and turns toward repentance. Judas's guilt quite literally leads to death like Paul talks about in the 2 Corinthians passage. Peter's, on the other hand, leads to him breaking down in remorse. The Bible says he literally "wept bitterly" (Matt. 26:75).

But that's not where it ended. Peter turned his grief into action. How do we know? For starters, John 21:7 talks about Peter running through the sea to embrace Jesus upon seeing him for the first time after the resurrection. And second, because in the rest of the New Testament we see Peter becoming one of the most ardent defenders of Christ. He didn't wallow in his guilt; he used it as fuel to run toward Jesus.

Can you see the difference? Judas sat in his shame, and it quite literally killed him. Peter wept over his sin, and it led him back to Jesus, toward transformation, and inspired him to spread the gospel to countless others. What you do after realizing your sin makes all the difference.

"Repentance is . . . actively turning from a false way of being, to a true one in Jesus again and again," Chandler explains.[12]

Worldly guilt leaves us isolated and stuck. Godly guilt throws us back into the arms of Jesus because we recognize he is the only one who can help us. And I can't think of a better place to be once you fully and truly realize the depths of what you've done. Why? Because shame is a liar, but in the presence of Jesus we are reminded of the truth. A truth that leads to peace despite our circumstances.

"Shame will tell you that you're the sum of your failures," Pastor Ian Simkins says. "Jesus says something profoundly different."[13]

Thank God. It's time we started listening.

SEVEN

Messy Sanctification

> This life, therefore, is not righteousness but growth in righteousness, not health but healing, not being but becoming, not rest but exercise. We are not yet what we shall be, but we are growing toward it. The process is not yet finished but it is going on. This is not the end but it is the road. All does not yet gleam in glory but all is being purified.
>
> —Martin Luther, "Defense and Explanation of All the Articles" in *Luther's Works*

I sat outside the gym, waiting for the doors to open.

I had started attending an early-morning fitness class that was the gym's first one of the day. Those of us who hate being late would show up even before the first employees and engage in small talk.

On this particular morning, three of us men got to chatting. The conversation went something like this:

Guy #1: "Jon and I go to the same church, actually."
Guy #2: "Oh, really? That's neat."

Messy Sanctification

Guy #1:   "Yeah. You should try it sometime."
Guy #2:   "Nah. I don't think they'd let someone like me in. I got some cleaning up to do."

If you're reading this and you're a Christian, no doubt there's a part of you saying something like, "No! That's the point. You get to come as you are! You don't have to get clean before you meet Jesus."

But consider this: I'd find out later that Guy #2 was, in fact, already a Christian. He wasn't a rowdy partier who was out sowing his wild oats. In fact, he was a pretty successful middle-aged family man who believed in and followed Jesus. But he had a past. Maybe even a present. He was ashamed and had deemed himself too broken and too dirty to come back to church until he had worn his sackcloth and ashes long enough to feel like he had paid his penance.

But while, on the surface, we bristle at that, let me ask you this: Are you part of a church / denomination / faith community that takes this approach with people who have messed up—especially messed up big? Do *you* take the same approach with those who are followers of Jesus who have messed up—especially messed up big? Do you take that same approach with *yourself* when you've messed up—especially messed up big? Sure, maybe you keep attending church. But have you drawn back from Jesus mentally, emotionally, or spiritually because you feel like you have some "cleaning up to do" before you come back to him?

That's what Adam and Eve did. They ran and hid. And I think it's what *we* do. After all, it's baked into sin's DNA to separate us from God. But we don't just do it with ourselves. We push others in that direction too, precisely *because* we do it to ourselves. It's like some twisted version of the Golden Rule: *I beat myself up, so I'm going to beat you up. I think I'm unworthy, so you must be made to feel unworthy too.*

It's all because so many of us fail to understand or embrace messy sanctification. We're quick to say, "Come as you are," but we forget (or ignore) that the gospel is just as much about "Stay as you become." We're gung ho about salvation, but we fall silent when it comes to sanctification. We fail to preach it and live it out for others, and we fail to preach it and live it out for ourselves.

And yet God wants you to embrace this process (see 2 Cor. 3:18; 1 Thess. 4:3a; 5:23–24).

That's why if there is only one concept that you take away from this book, I hope it's this idea of messy sanctification. I believe with every fiber of my being that if the church and its members were to embrace this doctrine—and actually live like they embrace it—we would see people turning toward Jesus like never before. And I'm not just talking about unbelievers turning to Jesus—I'm talking about believers *returning* to Jesus as well.

I was—and am—one of them. So are you. Because we all are.

Revisiting Sanctification

Let's recap what sanctification is. In its simplest form, sanctification is the process of becoming more like Jesus. It's ongoing. The day you become a Christian, your sanctification process begins. And spoiler alert: It never ends. As I mentioned earlier, salvation is a lifeline; sanctification is a lifetime.

But not only is sanctification becoming more like Jesus, it's also the process of becoming more aware of your sin. They go hand in hand, really. You *will* become more aware of your sin the closer you get to Jesus. But I want to call it out because I don't want you to be surprised when, as you embark on your own journey, you start noticing just how much you have to work on beyond whatever your immediate struggle is. That's normal.

I continue to be made aware of what I would now call glaring weaknesses in my life. And yet there are issues I see as weaknesses today that weren't even on my radar a year ago. Why? Because I'm becoming more and more aware of *all* the sin I need to fight as I draw nearer to Jesus. The closer we get to the light, the more we see the monsters that have been lurking in the shadows all along. As a Christian, then, you need to be comfortable with continual sin awareness. That's why famous Puritan preacher John Owen can say, "Be killing sin, or it will be killing you."[1] You and I will never run out of sins to kill. Never. It's ongoing. Forever.

Scripture makes this clear in a fascinating way that not many realize, by the way. In Romans 6:6, Paul says, "We know that our old self was crucified with him in order that the body of sin might be brought to nothing, so that we would no longer be enslaved to sin."

But do you know the word Paul uses in Greek for "brought to nothing"? It's *katargeō*. That's an interesting word choice. It certainly can be translated into harsh terms like "destroyed," as the King James Version and New Revised Standard Version do, or even "done away with," as the New American Standard Bible and New International Version do. But the Christian Standard Bible translates it as "rendered powerless" while the Literal Standard Version uses "made useless," or it can be—as one translator puts it—"rendered progressively weaker."[2] In other words, the actual word Paul uses is a term that doesn't *necessarily* denote an abrupt stoppage or complete destruction but rather can signal progress—an ongoing process of weakening something that still remains. Here's the point: What if "brought to nothing" is really about the ongoing *process* of incapacitating sin, not destroying it completely? Because we can't.

Yes, the old self died. Yes, the old self was crucified. But also—in what you might just have to chalk up to a mystery of the faith—that's actually something that isn't complete this side of glory. Sin has ultimately been destroyed, and yet it needs to be killed daily. There's an "ongoing 'crucifixion' which we ourselves do to our sinful nature, as we put to death the old nature within us," Tim Keller says.[3] Thus, when you factor in how Paul talks about our sin struggles throughout all of his letters, I think the "progressively

151

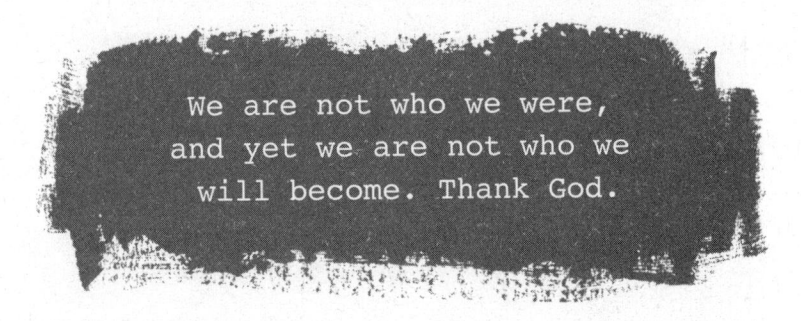

> We are not who we were, and yet we are not who we will become. Thank God.

weaker" translation is the best one—and it accurately reflects the sanctification process.

Still, we all seem to struggle with the "myth" that "once converted, fully converted," as Brennan Manning rightly points out.[4] The truth? "We have been saved. We are being saved. We work out our salvation. And we will be saved," David Powlison explains in his book, *How Does Sanctification Work?*[5]

We are not who we were, and yet we are not who we will become. Thank God.

Killing and Filling

When it comes to sanctification, it's actually made up of two distinct elements. They are mortification and vivification. Fancy words. But in reality, you can translate them into "killing" and "filling."*

Mortification is the killing aspect. It's what Owen is talking about in his quote. We need to be waging war on our sin and constantly rooting it out.

But the other aspect is vivification, the filling part. See, if we kill off sin but don't replace it with what's good and right, we're left empty. It's not enough to run away from something; we have to

---

* I'm thankful to Brett Smith of the Gospel Recovery Network for his training on this concept.

run toward something. Jesus himself talks about this concept in Matthew 12, when he tells the story of an unclean spirit leaving a person only to return with even more spirits when it "finds the house empty" (Matt. 12:44).

In fact, we even see it in the most direct verse on drunkenness in the Bible: "And do not get drunk with wine, for that is debauchery, *but* be filled with the Spirit" (Eph. 5:18, emphasis added). That "but" is important.

Think of it like weeding and feeding your lawn. Killing the weeds doesn't mean much if you neglect to water and fertilize your grass. The lawn will still burn up. Your soul is the same. We need to be killing the things that pull us away from Christ, and we need to be cultivating those things that draw us toward him. Our souls will go dry if we don't.

Here's an example from my own journey: I have always loved country music. Growing up in rural Wisconsin, I've listened to it for as long as I can remember. But after getting sober, I just haven't been able to listen to it. I've tried, but I just can't. Why? Two reasons.

First, I've become keenly aware of how much drinking culture has invaded country music. I always knew it was there, but now it's seemingly part of every song.

Second, I just have a stronger desire to think about, be surrounded by, and marinate in music that speaks to and uplifts my soul. That feels a little foreign. Growing up, my stepdad would force us to listen to Christian radio stations and punish us for tuning to anything but them. Now? The first three presets on my truck radio are all Christian stations.

Am I saying that you can't listen to country music if you're serious about your sobriety? Absolutely not. But what I am saying is that as the process of sanctification plays out, you may be surprised what your own mortification and vivification look like.

I have been.

It's for the Big Things Too

OK, so maybe you're all on board with sanctification. You get it. You want it. You support it. But do you *really*? See, when it comes to sanctification, there's something I think we have a hard time completely accepting: Sanctification is not just for the little sins; it's for the big sins too.

Even though we may say we get that, a lot of us don't live like we do when it comes down to it. We ostracize, we avoid, we gossip about, and we look down on the big sinners. Too many times when we talk (or sing) about God using broken people, we're OK with the people whose brokenness is the result of something that happened *to* them, but we hold our noses around those whose brokenness is a result of something they've caused *themselves*.

The words of the great theologian Dietrich Bonhoeffer should humble us:

> The pious fellowship permits no one to be a sinner. So everyone must conceal his sin from himself and from their fellowship. We dare not be sinners. Many Christians are unthinkably horrified when a real sinner is suddenly discovered among the righteous. So we remain alone with our sin, living in lies and hypocrisy. The fact is that we are sinners![6]

Here's the reality: The gospel of Jesus recognizes that we are not just sinners when we come to Jesus, but we will *continue* to be sinners even after he calls us.* Not just little sinners. Not just people who curse in traffic or tell a white lie to get out of a social commitment or get really mad at our kids after a long day. Those are the sins that we're OK admitting and struggling with.

But the big ones?

The adultery.

---

* Read Romans 6–8.

The rape.

The murder.

The abuse.

The addiction.

The abandonment.

The stealing.

The destruction.

No, those are different, we tell ourselves (and others), sometimes verbally but most of the time with either our silence or our actions. Our inactions, even.

Are there bigger, more vivid consequences for those sins? Absolutely! On one hand, I roll my eyes a little when people say there are no degrees of sin. Trust me, the domestic abuser will pay a bigger price here on earth than the person who fibs about their weekend plans so they can curl up by the fireplace instead of going to a concert.

On the other hand, sin is sin. No matter what it is, it separates us from God. And the point is, we are all infected with it. No one got the vaccine and is inoculated. And in eternity, the price for lying is the same as the price for murder.

But the gospel is that Jesus forgives it all. He forgives the miscue, the misstep, *and* he forgives the murder. And he forgives the alcoholic.

Even the Christian one.

"No one is so good that they don't need the grace of the gospel, nor so bad that they can't receive the grace of the gospel," Tim Keller says.[7]

That's why I call it messy sanctification. It involves the "big" things. The really hard issues. The disgusting acts. And we are all one anger-fueled decision, one wild night, one stupid mistake away from becoming one of those people. If we're not already.

It's the refrain of the ancient desert monks who, upon seeing someone else stumble, would remind themselves, "He today; I tomorrow."[8] There's a reason why that's tattooed on my left arm now. It's the humility I'm striving for every day. Since being made so vividly aware of my own sin and addictive personality, now when I hear of something particularly harsh or disturbing, I don't catch myself saying, "How could they?" Instead, I whisper, "That could be me."

You Can Still Be Used

One of the hardest things for me to reconcile regarding my time spent in active addiction is, in a sense, my double life.

How could I be struggling in secret while helping others so publicly? Does the fact that I was secretly sinning negate everything I was saying about and doing for Jesus? Are the truths contained in my past writing moot?

I've answered some of that up to this point, but there's one aspect I need you to hear and that I need to make abundantly clear. It's this: God uses broken people. He uses sinners.

I don't just mean people who have small flaws. I mean he uses sex addicts, murderers, liars, cheats, and anyone else you can imagine. And he even uses them *while* they're actively struggling. How do I know? Because, friend, while we are free from the eternal consequences of our sin, we do not stop sinning the moment we begin following Jesus. There is no theologian who will tell you that. Freedom "from" sin means we are free from its eternal consequences, it does not mean we stop sinning. Even the greatest saint was an ongoing sinner.

But too often we fail to live like it. We fail to live like it with others, and we fail to live like it with ourselves. And yet, we need to be reminding ourselves of it every single day—not only to keep ourselves humble but to keep ourselves from shame.

"What you see in the Bible isn't clean and stable lives, but messy, complicated, broken people with God right in the middle of every day—sustaining, encouraging, and reminding them of His grace," Matt Chandler explains.[9]

That's the story of the Bible. Messy, complicated, and broken people being used by God. Not just *formerly* messy people but *currently* messy people. *Future* messy people.

Here are some examples:

- Noah, after exiting the ark, got so drunk he lost his clothes. And yet he went on to live 350 more years (see Gen. 9:20–23).
- Abraham disobeyed God numerous times and demonstrated a lack of faith. And yet God was still faithful to make him the father of a "great nation"—even fulfilling his covenant when Abraham did not (see Gen. 12–16).
- Moses murdered a man, tried to reject the Lord's call on his life, and was even severely punished for disobeying God. And yet he found "favor" with God and was even granted the rare honor of seeing Yahweh (see Exod. 2:11–15; 33:1–23; Num. 20:1–13; Deut. 3:23–29).
- Rahab, despite being a non-Jewish prostitute, recognized God's authority and saved Joshua's spies, allowing them to take Jericho. She would later be welcomed as a Jew, and Matthew lists her in the lineage of Jesus. An obedient prostitute became a grandmother to the Messiah (see Josh. 2; Matt. 1:1–16).
- David was at minimum an adulterer and a murderer, but it seems pretty clear his actions with Bathsheba should be described as rape instead of the more palatable "affair."[10] And yet God's favor and anointing were upon him. Jesus

would later come from David's lineage (see 2 Sam. 11–12; 1 Kings 9:4–5).

- John the Baptist—who leapt in utero at just being near Jesus, who baptized Jesus, and who watched the Holy Spirit descend on Jesus—doubts near the end of his life whether Jesus really is the Messiah (see Luke 7:18–35). And yet Jesus says that "among those born of women none is greater than John" (v. 28).

- The apostle Peter, who was one of Jesus's most revered apostles, became so fearful of persecution he denied Jesus three times. And yet, knowing this would happen, Jesus nicknamed Peter the "rock" (see Matt. 16:18; 26:69–75; John 1:42). Peter was also rebuked by Paul for engaging in racist behavior, and yet he retained his ministry (see Gal. 2).

- The apostle Paul persecuted the early church "violently and tried to destroy it" (Gal. 1:13) and participated in the public execution of the disciple Stephen. He called himself the chief of sinners. And yet he became Christ's most ardent defender and preacher (see Acts 7–9; 1 Tim. 1:15).

"To this we could add that John Calvin participated in burning a man at the stake, Martin Luther made racist comments, George Whitefield and Jonathan Edwards owned slaves, John Wesley was an absentee husband, and more," pastor and author Scott Sauls writes.[11]

If messy sanctification applies to all these people, it applies to me. God may hate my sin, but he isn't limited by it.* I continually remind myself that while I was getting drunk and making an idol out of escapism, Jesus was still using me. That doesn't create pride in me; it creates great humility.

---

* For a deeper discussion, see this article by John Piper: https://www.desiringgod.org/interviews/does-sin-have-a-necessary-place-in-gods-plan-for-the-universe.

That applies to you too. He *has* used you despite your struggles. He *is* using you despite your struggles. And he *will* use you despite your struggles. This idea isn't some fringe concept. It's preached and embraced by countless others. Consider the following:

- Matt Chandler: "God pulls from the fringes of darkness those who will be powerful lights."[12]
- Tim Keller: "The gospel gives us a pair of spectacles through which we can review our own lives and see God preparing us and shaping us, even through our own failures and sins, to become vessels of His grace in the world."[13]
- Brennan Manning: "Jesus comes not for the super-spiritual but for the wobbly and the weak-kneed who know they don't have it all together, and who are not too proud to accept the handout of amazing grace."[14]
- Paul David Tripp: "The Bible is not a collection of stories of human heroes. No, the Bible is the story of a hero Redeemer who transforms weak and ordinary people by his powerful grace."[15]

That's you. That's me. That's all of us.

You have not messed up too much. You are not messed up too much. Your family history and trauma are not too messed up. You are not too far gone. Whatever you've done while drunk can be, and already has been, forgiven. Everything I'm saying here applies to you. Yes, *you*. The mark of a mature (or maturing) Christian isn't whether you're sinning or not; it's where, what, and who you're running to *when* you sin.

Rest in this: Many times what we are most qualified to talk and write about are the things we continue to struggle with. Why? Because we know them intimately. The idea that we preach against our worst sin doesn't have to be an indictment. It's an indicator of grace.

While working on this chapter I met with a friend who had recently transitioned from being a pastor to a full-time counselor. I told him about my struggle to reconcile how God still used me despite my drinking problem. He asked me something that floored me.

"You know Eugene Peterson struggled with alcohol, right?"

"You're kidding!" I said in disbelief.

Peterson is the deep thinker responsible for *The Message* paraphrase of the Bible, as well as the insanely popular book *A Long Obedience in the Same Direction*. If you imagine an elderly, straight-laced, professorial saint who doesn't struggle with alcohol, the picture that comes to mind is probably Peterson.

As soon as I got home, I googled what my friend had told me. And sure enough, in a review of his biography, there it was: "Though Peterson lived a remarkably disciplined life, he continued to struggle with an 'old nemesis,' his evening practice of drinking alcohol."[16]

Friend, God uses us despite our struggles.

Why Repentance Matters

But Jon, what about repentance? What about remorse? What about the godly guilt you talked about last chapter? Does any of that matter when it comes to messy sanctification?

I'm glad you asked. I don't pretend to be a theologian who can fully unpack the breadth of everything written on forgiveness and repentance, but there are three things we need to understand about it.

First off, we see how important repentance is when we look at salvation. In fact, repentance is the first step of salvation. "Repent, for the kingdom of heaven is at hand," Jesus says in Matthew 4:17. Peter echoes this in Acts 2:38: "Repent and be baptized every one of you in the name of Jesus Christ for the forgiveness of your sins." Repentance and salvation go hand in hand.

Second, if repentance is important for salvation—for coming to Jesus—it follows, then, that it's also important for *returning* to Jesus.* That's sanctification. In other words, repentance isn't just a onetime thing. No, *continued* repentance after salvation is part of—and necessary for—our sanctification journeys. And as you become more like Jesus and get closer to him, you can't help but repent because you become more keenly aware of your shortcomings. Repent when you come to Jesus the first time, yes, but then repent when you return to him every time after that.

That brings us to the third thing: When we repent and return to Jesus, it makes restoration and reconciliation possible with those around us. Repentance is the necessary ingredient for those, in fact. That's the aspect I really want to focus on because it's especially important for our situations.

Take the biblical examples we covered earlier. When the person was repentant, that's when we see a restored relationship with God and those around them. We see this in the story of David, for example. After being confronted about what he did to Bathsheba and her husband, he is grieved, repents, and is restored (see 2 Sam. 12). In fact, Psalm 51 is all about David grieving and repenting over his sin.

I've experienced that in my own life. When I was finally broken enough about my drinking, my sin, and what it was doing to me, my family, and my relationship with Jesus, I experienced a genuine remorse that led to repentance. That repentance then birthed restoration and reconciliation with God and others that tastes better than any bourbon or beer I have ever experienced (and I've experienced a lot of them).

I'm reminded of my friend Sarah here. She's a Christian woman who, despite her faith, cheated on her husband with his best friend.

---

* Every act of sin is a turning away from God, after all.

As a result of her repentance, though, she and her husband reconciled and now have five incredible boys.*

The point is, there's something greater waiting for you on the other side of repentance and remorse—true repentance and true remorse that necessitate action like we talked about last chapter in relation to godly guilt. It's like some cosmic chemistry formula: God takes our mistakes and our messes, combines them with our repentance, remorse, and Jesus, and the result is a reconciliation more amazing than we could have ever imagined.

"God's response to true confession is always grace and mercy," author Jamie Winship writes. That's the truth. But it gets even better. "When you live in continuous confession and repentance, your life is transformed in every area: professionally, spiritually, physically. In every way, you begin to ascend," he adds.[17]

Reconciliation, restoration, and transformation. That's what's waiting for you on the other side of repentance.

Three Caveats

I want to be clear on three things as we conclude this chapter, though. The first is that there are cases where, even though someone may repent, reconciliation and restoration with those they've hurt is not possible or even wise barring the miraculous. I'm thinking of cases involving trauma, especially of a sexual nature or involving children.

That doesn't mean forgiveness isn't possible. It means the relationship has been too fractured by sin and the consequences are too great for things to be like they were before. That's the reality of sin and brokenness, and we shouldn't try to forcefully rebuild what is too broken to be put back together—especially when it would involve retraumatizing victims.

---

* You can read about her journey in her book, *Desert Vineyards: A Story of Bulimia, Adultery, and Infertility Redeemed by Truth*.

Second, there are still consequences for our actions. We see that in David's story. The child he conceived with Bathsheba died as a result of the sinful way he was conceived (see 2 Sam. 12:14). Friend, I don't say this flippantly: There are some things in your life that may never be the same as the result of what was conceived in sin. And yet the freedom that's possible as a result of your repentance is still worth it.

The third thing I want to make clear is that sanctification and grace do not give us an excuse. We can't intentionally keep sinning and say, "God is all about grace. We're all being sanctified, so it's no big deal." Romans 6 makes this abundantly clear. Sanctification is not a "get out of jail free" card.*

In fact, God's grace is not all rainbows and butterflies. Sometimes his grace looks like him giving us over to our sinful desires. "God's care can be violent," Paul David Tripp reminds us. "He rips you from what is dangerous to give you what is better."[18]

Unfortunately, we've seen plenty of prominent Christian leaders who have forgotten this. Instead of being repentant, too many of them have looked for excuses, they've hidden behind bravado and blamed cancel culture, or they've tried to cover up what needs to be dragged into the light. Sanctification may explain their actions, but it doesn't excuse them. And yet some of them have tried to use it to do just that.

On the other hand, the leaders who have experienced restoration—which, again, does not mean a canceling out of all consequences—are the ones who have owned their messes. They did not hide. They did not make excuses. They did not get defensive. They took action. And you see clear evidence around them that they underwent a change.

That begs the question: Does someone with a messy sanctification story *have* to prove that they are truly repentant? And if so, to whom?

---

* The truth is you may still actually have to go to jail for some of the things you do while being sanctified.

The answer to the first question is yes. But that's not as prescriptive as it sounds. I like to think of it as the offender *gets* to show they are repentant. See, true repentance is naturally external anyway because it leads to action. That means there can't *not* be evidence. We will see humility, confession, and brokenness.

As to the second question, in my experience the people most likely to know when there has been true repentance and change are those who are closest to the offender. The husband, the wife, the children, the friends, the pastors, the elders.

Let me explain how this played out in my own life.

I'll never forget when, a few months into my sobriety journey, Brett and I were hosting some good friends of ours for a game night. We were telling them how I had been doing intensive therapy to get to the root cause of my escapism. Without prompting, Brett spoke up: "He's a different person. Sometimes I don't recognize him."

I literally did one of those wide-eyed eyebrow raises you see in the movies. *Did she really just say that?* I wasn't offended; I was surprised. I knew I had been making strides, and I knew I both felt different and was acting differently, but I didn't realize it had become so obvious to others—especially to the person closest to me.

It had.

We don't get that benefit with everyone we see fall publicly. But we can look for signs. Are they defensive? Haughty? Humble? What are those closest to them saying about their transformation?

Because, in the end, there are no shortcuts through repentance. You can quickly embrace it, but you can't rush through it. My prayer, though, is that you pursue it and experience it no matter how long it takes. Because it's more than worth it.

PART 3

BREAKING FREE

EIGHT

Finding Sobriety

> Sobriety isn't the same thing as not drinking. You can be as dry as the Gobi Desert and still be a slave to alcoholic thinking.
> —Heather Kopp, *Sober Mercies*

Now that I've shared and dissected my story, I want to empower you to change your own. I don't care what you've done, what Rubicon you've crossed, or how bleak it looks. There is hope. You can have freedom.

That's where the four steps I took come in: abiding, finding your true identity, practicing radical vulnerability, and obeying. However, I want to be clear about some things before I unpack them.

First, "freedom" doesn't mean you won't still struggle. Paul had a continual "thorn in his flesh" (see 2 Cor. 12:7–10). I still struggle with anxiety, OCD, and a desire to escape. But that's the key: I'm *struggling* with them. I'm aware of them and I'm actively taking steps with God to combat them. And with these four steps, I've experienced a greater freedom from them than ever before.

Second, these steps (and how I talk about them) are *a* way to pursue freedom, but they are not the only way. And yet, there is no doubt that as Christians we should be practicing each one of them. We need to abide in Christ, we need to get our identity from him, we need to practice radical vulnerability, and we need to do what he says. So in that sense, none of them are optional.

Third, I view these steps as bedrock. What I mean is that they go even deeper than a foundation. They are what a foundation is built on. Whatever pathway of recovery you choose or whatever additional steps God tells you to take while reading these, build upon these steps. They are an amalgamation of Scripture, Bible study, intense prayer, writings from people wiser than me, therapy, counsel, science, research, and experience.

Fourth, these steps are generally a progression. You abide, then you find your identity, then you are radically vulnerable, and then you take steps of obedience. However, the only hard-and-fast "rule" is that you start with abiding. You have to. If you're not spending time with Jesus, how can you ever hear his voice? From there, maybe you will hear a clear step of obedience before you practice radical vulnerability. That's OK.

Fifth, these steps assume you are either a Christian, conversant in Christianity, or curious about Christianity. Why? Because they require trust in Jesus. That will make sense in a minute.

Sixth, these steps don't *exclude* things like AA, counseling, therapy, treatment, or Celebrate Recovery. For example, maybe one of those is a practical application of the third or fourth step that you're about to see. Trauma therapy was a big part of my own step 3.

Seventh, there's room for individuality. These steps are universal, but they are deeply personal. Your abiding time can look different from mine; your specific identity will look different from mine; how you practice radical vulnerability can look different from how I practice it; and while some of our steps of obedience will overlap, the specific commands will likely look different.

Eighth, I don't pretend to have "invented" these steps. Christians have been practicing them for thousands of years. I'm just putting them together nice and succinct for you.

And finally, you don't just go through these steps once. It's a continual process. Abide always, constantly steep in your identity, continually practice radical vulnerability, and pursue obedience your entire life.

But before we unpack these steps, I need to be honest about something first because it comes up frequently.

AA and Twelve-Step Recovery

When you hear the word *sober* or *sobriety*, what comes to mind?

I wouldn't be surprised if you thought about Alcoholics Anonymous. That's because AA, as it's known, is by far the most successful recovery program in history and the one most people associate with getting sober. Since its founding in 1935, it has helped over two million people.[1] It relies on the Twelve Steps and regular meetings to take the addict on a journey of healing.

And I need to be honest about why I never fully participated.

In fact, I didn't follow any twelve-step program (there are others). I did read the AA handbook—or the "Big Book," as it's called—and found it useful in some ways, but that's as far as I went.

I struggled with how detailed I should get in explaining why, because my heart is not to dissuade anyone from using a tool that is available to find sobriety, which AA is.* In fact, many use AA meetings as a great gateway into recovery before pursuing other methods. But I believe I owe it to you to let you know why I didn't do it that way. And there are two main reasons.

---

* That said, I am a more ardent advocate for alternative twelve-step programs that are grounded in Jesus, like Celebrate Recovery.

Reason 1

The first reason has to do with identity. As you'll see in just a bit, identity is a very important part of my recovery journey. I think it's crucial for everyone's, in fact. Because of that, I struggled with the traditional way you introduce yourself at an AA meeting.

"My name is Jon, and I'm an alcoholic."

That just never felt right to me. Why? Because it feels like I'm rooting my identity in the worst decisions and period of my life. Why does "alcoholic" have to be my identity forever?*

Instead, I want my past decisions to *describe* me, not *define* me. And something within me said that when I got on the other side of this period, my identity was going to be different. It would change. It would be cemented and rooted in something else. Yes, I use the term *alcoholic* at times now, but for one, I'm not being forced to. (And remember, it's a part of me, not the whole me.) I get to use it on my terms and because I know that using it helps the greatest number of people quickly understand my condition before I unpack it. But I can—and may—cease to use it at any time. And I get to make that choice.

Second, when I use the term, I use it with all the nuance I've come to appreciate. I understand the AUD spectrum and how it's not binary anymore. Back when I started this journey, though? I didn't know what I know now, so the idea of *having* to use it bothered me.

So I read the AA material, took some helpful insights, but chose not to attend formal meetings or do the Steps.†

That said, I've learned since then that while introducing yourself as an alcoholic at each meeting is practiced by many, it's technically

---

* Yes, I know I use the term in the title of this book. But as I said in chapter 2, the point of that was to both be attention-grabbing and then guide you through how we have to reframe and reuse the term.

† However, I've had several Twelve-Step adherents who have read early copies of this book point out that I actually did do the Twelve Steps naturally. Go figure!

> I want my past decisions to describe me, not define me.

not required. But I didn't have the benefit of that information at the time.

Reason 2

The second reason I never fully participated in AA is because of the uncomfortable skepticism I received from some for not following the program. That turned me off.

For example, when I first started telling the world about my recovery journey, I had someone send me a curious and slightly scolding message asking what my "sponsor"—which in AA is a long-term accountability partner—thought about my sobriety writings. When I asked this person to explain more, they responded that their recovery was "the most important thing" in their life and that they didn't make any significant moves regarding alcohol without talking to their sponsor. The implication was clear: Unless I have an AA sponsor approving my writing, I should keep quiet.

But that comment also made something else clear: I see my sobriety and recovery differently. How? Sobriety and recovery are *not* the most important things in my life. They shouldn't be. And because of my faith, they can't be. Remember, a disorder (especially in the Christian sense) is all about misordered priorities. The moment I treat sobriety and recovery as the most important things in my life is the moment I start flirting with losing them. Why? Because sobriety and recovery, like anything, can and will disappoint. If

I'm looking to them for fulfillment, what happens when they stop being fulfilling? Because, honestly, sometimes they're not that fun!

Today, the freedom I've found *includes* sobriety and recovery, but they're the result of properly ordering my life around Jesus. They're the benefit, not the goal! By finding Jesus, I found myself, I found my family, I found sobriety, and I found recovery. And by taking that approach, I got the most fulfilled, most abundant life.

That really cannot make sense to people who aren't fully following Jesus or aren't at least interested in following Jesus. I get that. But it's the truth.

"Christians prone to alcoholism may not need fewer AA meetings, but they will need more than AA meetings," Tony Reinke, cohost with John Piper of the *Ask Pastor John* podcast, writes. He continues, quoting Piper: "If it helps, 'give thanks to God for his great grace in using AA.' But then press into the gospel, because 'Jesus shed his blood to deliver alcoholics and the rest of us from whatever bondage holds us fast' (Titus 2:14)."[2] To that end, AA is a way to get sober, but it is not "the Way" or the only way. It may not even be the best way. Either way, it's a tool, not the goal. Use it if you need to, but never worship it or *any* program for that matter. Reserve that for Jesus.

The Four Steps

Instead of focusing on what I *didn't* do, I really want to home in on what I did do. And that leads me to the four steps. Let me remind you: I didn't hit my rock-bottom moment and then come up with these. They didn't come to me in a vision or a dream. Rather, when I was finally in a healthy place, during my abiding time I looked back and started taking notes on what I had done—and that's when they emerged. They are inherently spiritual, but they are also action-oriented and practical. Each one will get its own chapter in this section, but I want to give you an overview first.

Step 1: Abiding in Christ

It was May 2023 when Brett and I went on our abiding retreat in Georgia that focused on learning how to fight for and spend time with Jesus daily. Within two days, I admitted for the first time that I had a disordered relationship with alcohol.

Why?

Because, once again, when we get really serious about getting closer to Jesus, we can't help but recognize where we are falling short. Our imperfections become clearer. The light can't help but expose the darkness. He reveals the junk in our lives—and the extent to which that junk affects us and those around us.

In the end, abiding is about daily dependence on God for daily guidance from God. It isn't about thinking your way out of, or through, your problems. It's about listening your way through them and trusting that God—and what he's telling you—is enough.

Practically, that abiding looks like actually spending time with Jesus. Novel, I know. But remember, it's surprising what we Christians can know and fail to do. That's why now, nearly every morning after I get up, I journal, I pray, I read, and then I listen to God. Sometimes it lasts thirty minutes, but most times it lasts much longer. I keep going until I'm filled up and until I sense that I am released to go about my day.* As Martin Luther apparently once said, "I have so much to do that I must spend the first three hours in prayer."†

Freedom from alcohol for me started by abiding. And it's the foundation on which everything else is built.

---

* Don't worry, you don't have to start there. In fact, your abiding time can even look different from mine. We'll talk about that more in chapter 9.
† The origin of the quote is unclear. Charles Spurgeon popularized it by attributing it to Luther, but it is not found in any of Luther's original texts.

Step 2: Finding Your True Identity

Once I started abiding with Jesus consistently and understanding who God is, I had to understand who I was. Not who I thought I was but who God created me to be. Very specifically. That means I had to find my identity.

Sure, many of us have heard that we have to "find our identity in Christ." That's true. But that's not what I'm talking about here, or at least that's not the *only* thing I'm talking about here. I'm talking about the very specific identity that God has given you.

We all have one. It's the combination of things like passion, calling, and skill. And once you seek it and God reveals it to you, your life takes on new meaning. You receive a new level of clarity. You are empowered and energized not only to pursue what's best but also to leave behind what's dragging you down.

Step 3: Practicing Radical Vulnerability

My third step was practicing radical vulnerability. Not regular vulnerability—*radical* vulnerability. That's a very important and intentional descriptor.

By now, we've all heard we need to be vulnerable. Our sins, our struggles, breed and fester in darkness. The devil loves it when we keep them hidden, then. Vulnerability brings them into the light, opens the wounds, and lets healing begin. It helps break the power of whatever we're struggling with.

But here's the problem: We've become used to regular vulnerability.

Here's an example: My son has chronic ear infections. Because of that, the antibiotics that used to work for him don't really work anymore. So, what happens when he *does* need antibiotics? The doctor prescribes something that the bacteria isn't used to. Something more powerful. Why? Because our diseases, our infections, are smart. They get used to whatever we throw at them.

That's the difference between *regular* vulnerability and *radical* vulnerability. Our sinful natures have gotten used to regular vulnerability and know how to skirt around it. They know how to outsmart it. So we need something more powerful.

Radical vulnerability is the prescription. It isn't just bringing our struggles to light; it's dragging them out kicking and screaming and then yelling for the world to look at them. It's exposing them in an uncomfortable way. And it's a key to finding freedom.

By the way, do you know another name for radical vulnerability? *True confession.* And the Bible is clear about the cleansing power of true confession (see 1 John 1:9).

Step 4: Obeying What God Tells You to Do

My final step was obeying. Put plainly, obeying is doing what God tells us to do through prayer and being committed to what we know to be right and true (and what he tells us) through studying his Word. It's that simple. But it's that hard. Here's what that's looked like for me:

I've given things up.

I've started practicing important spiritual disciplines.

I've sent bold and even uncomfortable emails.

I've asked for forgiveness. A lot.

I've met with people I didn't want to meet with.

I've said no to things that appeared to be great opportunities.

And through that process, God has transformed me.

How? There is something internal that happens to us when we obey—especially when we obey the Creator of the universe. We get peace. We get clarity. We also start trusting God more. We can't help it.

That trust breeds something else: humility. And you know what you need to break free from your struggle? You need humility. Even AA tells its members to admit they are "powerless" and to turn themselves over to a "higher power." You and I just have the benefit of knowing who that higher power is.

The Initial Result

This is the part where I tell you how amazing my life got right after I took all these steps and especially immediately after getting sober.

Nope.

As I noted in the introduction, life was tough after I stopped drinking. It was dark, even.

Geez, Jon, don't make it so appealing.

Well, you need to know the truth. Because if you choose this path, you should do so knowing exactly what you're getting into. And in my experience, it was hard at first. There is no doubt that the years of a misordered/disordered relationship with alcohol had rewired my brain to a certain extent. I had lost my ability to cope healthily with the world around me. Even nominally anxiety-inducing moments had become an excuse to drink, which meant facing them without alcohol was rough. There were afternoons and evenings when I found myself literally pacing because I didn't know what to do with myself. That's because nearly everything had become "drinking and ____."

Drinking and watching TV.

Drinking and playing LEGO with my son.

Drinking and teaching my daughter to ride a bike.

Drinking and talking with Brett.

Drinking and cooking.

Drinking and opening Christmas presents.

Drinking and watching sports.

Drinking and working late.

So when I took away the drinking, I felt lost.

There were other things, like the headaches and especially the night sweats. There was also anxiety, pain (both physical and emotional), uncertainty, anger, overwhelm, and sadness. I literally had to grieve the death of a companion that had been with me through a lot.

For the first time in a long time, and in some cases for the first time ever, I was forced to sit with thoughts, feelings, emotions, and realities that I had tried so hard to run from. I was forced to confront traumas that sometimes made me overreact to the simplest comment or smallest disagreement in explosive ways. I was forced to be curious about my pains and my anger. I couldn't just drink them away.

Friend, that is not fun. It is necessary, but it is not fun. And yet, I am not alone in experiencing that. You are not alone in experiencing that. It's actually quite common.

"As you reduce your dependence on a numbing behavior, you'll likely notice new feelings that surface, vulnerable feelings that may be uncomfortable or unpleasant," Dr. Alison Cook warns. But remember her encouragement from chapter 5: "Those vulnerable feelings present you with a new opportunity to . . . brave a healthier way to care for yourself."[3]

That's what the four steps are: a healthier way to care for yourself. And as I practiced them, slowly but surely I began to reap the benefits.

How long did that take? Several months. My body, brain, and spirit were so out of whack from years of numbing and coping that it took time to reset. There were times I'd find myself angry for no reason, on edge, anxious. I even briefly tried the hemp gummies again a few months into my journey!* But eventually, through practicing the four steps, I found those things fading away.

I don't know how long that will take for you, but don't be shocked. A life with Jesus equals peace, *not* a piece of cake. The sooner we realize that, the quicker we'll find that true peace. I'm telling you it gets better.

The Benefits

Explaining the good that emerged when I followed the steps and quit drinking is hard to put into words. Why? Because it was both a physical and a spiritual experience.

I'm not trying to sound flowery or fluffy here, but there's something that happens to your body, your mind, and especially your spirit when your priorities are aligned like they should be. Or at least when one priority that has been so misordered for so long is put in its rightful place and Jesus is put back in *his* rightful one.

For starters, the shame I had experienced for so many years began turning into genuine repentance and remorse. A beautiful brokenness appeared—the kind of brokenness that gives up on trying to hold together what needs to be ripped apart, lays bare all your jagged parts, and offers them up to the One who knit you together in the first place. Humility—genuine humility—began to peek through.

I also started rediscovering aspects of myself that drinking had buried. I've heard others say this, and it's true: I became more present with, and for, the people I love most. I was able to live in the moment. I was able to give true and lasting attention to the things and especially the people that needed to be a priority. I'll

---

* The Lord convicted me that while I was still *technically* sober, I was once again trying to escape and turn to something other than him. So I gave them up.

never forget the conversation Brett and I had in early 2024, around nine months after my last drink, that solidified this for me. It still brings tears to my eyes today.

"I feel like I finally got the husband I always wanted," she said as we sat across from each other on the couch. "The one I wanted to marry."

Knife, meet heart.

In addition to a repaired relationship with Brett, other things started happening too. I can't fully describe how much more time I got back. Until I stopped drinking, I didn't realize how much time I spent thinking about it and planning for it. Days became longer in the best sense. They might as well have been thirty-six hours, not twenty-four.

With all the extra time, I also started experiencing a lot of practical benefits. For example, I became more productive in my consulting work. Even clients commented on the "new" me. I tell people that it was like I took a "limitless pill," a reference to the 2011 movie starring Bradley Cooper in which a mysterious pill allows him to use 100 percent of his brain capacity. My brain literally began functioning better, quicker. I felt more alive. I wasn't as easily distracted.

I also became a "yes man"—not in the worst sense but in the best sense. I began saying yes to so many more fun and healthy activities. I began going out with friends again. I attended more church events. We started going out to dinner more as a family. I was even a bad millennial and started taking and making more actual phone calls!

Additionally, I became a voracious reader, Brett and I binged as many shows as we could, and I began listening to books and podcasts to help me get to the roots of my struggles. My confidence grew. My personality, my demeanor, and my outlook started to change. My wonder returned. I found peace.

But none of those things compare to the spiritual benefits.

I can honestly say that I experienced the most rapid and rabid spiritual growth of my life in the first year of my sobriety. It was a true spiritual awakening. It's like everything I knew about Jesus, about God, about faith stopped being elusive and was right there for me to grab. It took on new meaning. My spiritual senses were heightened and even transformed. I could taste spiritual colors. I could see spiritual sounds. I could feel spiritual smells. I could hear spiritual pictures. I became so dependent on Jesus just to sleep—just to get through the night sweats, for example—that he became my everything.

I also started saying things about my faith and describing it in ways that would make young Jon snicker. If you were raised in the church, you likely know what I'm talking about. We all had those adults who would do or say things in relation to God that were anything but "cool." Now? I'm the one doing and saying things in relation to my spiritual life that look and sound "funny."

That's because desperation doesn't care about what sounds cool. And I was desperate. I threw myself on God and his grace. I begged for his mercy. I began to fully and completely believe that he loved me and cared for me because I knew what I fully deserved as a result of my sin and my drinking. And nothing makes you more desperate for someone outside yourself than seeing what's truly inside yourself.

That's where I was. I had come to the end of myself. I couldn't pretend anymore. I couldn't hide anymore. I couldn't do it anymore. I finally realized how much I needed Jesus.

That's why I've actually become thankful for this journey of messy sanctification. It has helped me understand the full gospel of Jesus Christ while also opening my eyes to so much truth. Like realizing that the very things alcohol promised to deliver are exactly what it took away:

It promised peace but gave me anxiety.

It promised bravery but gave me shame.

It promised fun but gave me regret.

It promised me a friend but left me alone.

It promised me more but gave me less.

It promised me freedom but gave me bondage.

By drawing closer to Jesus, by finding my identity in him, by practicing radical vulnerability, and by doing what he told me to do, I was able to see those lies for what they were. And I fell in love with him. Not just again, but maybe for the first time.

That doesn't mean I wasn't a Christian before. I was. I knew Jesus. I believed in Jesus. I liked Jesus and wanted more of Jesus. But I didn't understand what it meant to truly, deeply, and completely love Jesus until he was all I had to hold on to.

That's what I'm inviting you into today. Right now. If you have a misordered/disordered relationship with alcohol, or anything really, I truly believe that by taking these steps you will fall in love with him. I think it's impossible not to. And your life will be radically different because of that. Because of him.

In that sense, my sobriety journey isn't about going back to who I was before my misordered/disordered relationship with alcohol. It's about becoming who I was never able to become because of the growth my drinking stunted. I don't want to go back; I want to go forward. Because there's something even greater there than who I was before.

That's waiting for you too.

NINE

Abiding in Christ (Step 1)

> I seek God daily because I need to. When I don't meet God personally, thoughtfully, and humbly, I suffer the consequences. It's analogous to forgetting to eat. I suffer because I am hungry, not because I feel guilty.
>
> —David Powlison, *How Does Sanctification Work?*

I'm not the guy who should be writing a chapter on abiding with Christ. Seriously.

For my entire life, I've struggled with the idea of "quiet time." Being still always meant being lonely. Being silent always gave my thoughts, worries, and fears a megaphone. And being told to be quiet (or mostly quiet) sounded a lot like the hurtful comments of people trying to stifle my personality.

But therein lies part of my problem.

See, I think when a lot of us hear the term "abiding with Christ," we think it has to look one way—and that way, from what we've been led to believe, is hands folded, head down, Bible open. Sequestered. Silent. Somber. If we get fancy, it can look like us on our knees, praying out loud in the early mornings, or even welcoming the morning sun with some words from a devotional. But either way, it *has* to fit into a certain box with predetermined boundaries and expectations.

What a bunch of crap. Can I say that? I guess I just did.

But for most of my life I didn't know that. Sure, I'd heard some people whisper that abiding could look a little different. But for the most part they were viewed with a little side-eye and maybe even seen as somewhat less holy and less disciplined than those who started their morning with a very regimented and very purposeful "quiet time."

So, maybe not surprisingly, for most of my life I struggled with prayer. It never felt personal. It felt like an obligation, not an opportunity. Growing up, my stepdad even forced us to pray for set periods of time on a whim, and many times "in tongues." We couldn't do certain things until we finished.

Prayer was a punishment.

So the fact that I'm here, writing *this* chapter about abiding in Christ should tell you something. And that something is this: The single greatest step you can take toward changing your relationship with alcohol as a Christian is abiding with Christ. Whatever that looks like.

That's because intentional communion with Christ is the best foundation for change. Not just change of actions and attitudes but change of heart. Remember, you can address the fruit—you can stop drinking, cheating, or whatever else you're doing that's destructive—but the goal should be to kill the root. And as Christians, we know the only thing that can ultimately treat our root disease is Jesus.

That's why I want to be clear: You can find sobriety without Jesus. Countless people have. But I believe they're missing out. Why? Because they have not found the true peace, joy, and fulfillment that a life with Jesus offers.

> I believe that when it comes to healing trauma, addictions, and hurts, Christ—the great Healer—offers the best salve for the soul.

I don't just want sobriety. I want Christian sobriety because, well, I'm a Christian. And as a Christian, I believe that when it comes to healing trauma, addictions, and hurts, Christ—the great Healer—offers the best salve for the soul. I don't want a sobriety that's separate from my faith. I want a sobriety that integrates and celebrates my faith.

And that starts with abiding.

What Is Abiding?

The term *abiding* comes from John 15:1–11. Let's start by reading the words of Jesus together:

> I am the true vine, and my Father is the vinedresser. Every branch in me that does not bear fruit he takes away, and every branch that does bear fruit he prunes, that it may bear more fruit. Already you are clean because of the word that I have spoken to you. Abide in me, and I in you. As the branch cannot bear fruit by itself, unless it abides in the vine, neither can you, unless you abide in me. I am the vine; you are the branches. Whoever abides in me and I in him, he it is that bears much fruit, for apart from me you can do nothing. If anyone does not abide in me he is thrown away like a branch and withers; and the branches are gathered, thrown into the fire, and burned. If you abide in me, and my words abide in you, ask whatever you wish, and it will be done for you. By this my Father is glorified, that you bear much fruit and so prove to be my disciples. As the Father has loved me, so have I loved you. Abide

in my love. If you keep my commandments, you will abide in my love, just as I have kept my Father's commandments and abide in his love. These things I have spoken to you, that my joy may be in you, and that your joy may be full.

OK, there's a lot there. Whole books have been written on the topic of abiding, and I don't pretend to be a New Testament scholar who can unpack all of its richness. Instead, I'm going to focus on one specific idea: being in, and with, Jesus. It's the idea that we have access to the life-giving and life-sustaining person who created the universe. It's marinating in him. It's drawing closer to him. It's speaking to him and listening to him.

But even that doesn't fully do the term justice. In some ways, it's like trying to use a clunky English word to describe a beautiful foreign one. So let me tag four people in to help us.

The first is Jamie Winship. Winship's book *Living Fearless* has been life-changing for me. His work is focused mainly on finding your specific identity in Christ, which we'll talk about more in the next chapter, but ironically (or maybe not so) he opens his identity book by talking about the importance of abiding. After all, how are you going to download your identity if you're not hooked up to the identity giver?

Winship calls abiding "the process of personal observation and experience with Jesus."[1] There's that word *experience* again. Remember, in chapter 4 I had all the right theology and (mostly) right thinking, but I lacked a desire for—and the practice of—experiencing Jesus. Abiding is the key to that. It's not a formula; it's finding and practicing how you experience Jesus. Maybe that's through study, maybe that's through song, maybe that's through nature.

Our second guide to abiding is renowned pastor John Piper. He calls abiding "the act of receiving and trusting all that God is for us in Christ."[2] Trust and dependence go hand in hand. When you are dependent on someone, being with them isn't much of an option. It's less an obligation and more a necessity. A fish doesn't feel an "obligation" to stay in the water; it feels a pull toward it because there's an inherent understanding that water holds the key to life. It *needs* the water. Anything outside of it feels foreign. That's what healthy abiding feels like.

The third person who helps us understand abiding is pastor John Mark Comer. In his book *Practicing the Way*, he breaks down the actual word Jesus uses for *abide* in John 15, and it's really helpful:

> The word for "abide" is *menō* in Greek; it can be translated "remain" or "stay" or "dwell" or "make your home in." We could translate the verse like this: "Make your home in me, as I make my home in you." Jesus uses this word *menō* not once but *ten times* in this short teaching. . . . He's driving to a singular point: Make your home in my presence by the Spirit, and never leave.[3]

I love that. "Make your home in my presence." Think for a second what a home means (or maybe for some of you, what it *should* mean). It means safety, peace, comfort. It's where we spend the majority of our time. It's where we eat, sleep, and get clean. Now imagine Jesus being or providing all those things for your soul.

Our final guide is systematic theology professor Sinclair Ferguson. He describes abiding as "allowing [God's] word to fill our minds, direct our wills, and transform our affections."[4] That last part is really key. No doubt my affections were out of whack while I was in the thick of my misordered/disordered drinking. I wanted alcohol more than I wanted so many other things. But when I started practicing abiding, my affections changed. They were properly reordered.

All four of these definitions together, I think, give us a complete understanding of what it looks like to abide.*

---

* I intentionally brought these people together because they come from different backgrounds and evangelical perspectives. I think that's important and helpful.

It's experiencing Jesus.

It's making our home in Jesus.

It's receiving, trusting, and being dependent on Jesus.

It's marinating in Jesus so much that it transforms our affections.

Friend, that is so much more than a quiet time. "Quiet time" sells abiding short! Can you see that? Abiding is communion with God. Not just daily but constantly. It's how Paul can tell us to "pray without ceasing" (1 Thess. 5:17). I get it, that may seem daunting. But I'm not suggesting that in order to abide with Christ, every thought during every second of every day needs to be about Jesus. But that said, I do think it probably involves giving more thought, attention, and words to him than we do now. After all, we are immersed in a society obsessed with hustle and stealing our attention *away* from Jesus.

Comer gives us a test that I think is helpful to assess where we're at:

> When you first come awake at the beginning of the day, where does your mind naturally go? When you lay your head on your pillow after a long, tiring day, what are your final thoughts as you drift off to sleep? In the little moments of space throughout your day—waiting in line for your morning coffee, stuck in traffic, sitting down to a meal—where does your mind fall "without thinking" about it?[5]

The goal would be to answer all those questions with "to Jesus."

I say that's the goal. I'm not there. Gosh, no. My guess is you're not there either. But it's something to strive for. And it's something that isn't as impossible as you might think. How do I know? Because since getting sober, I've found myself able to answer "to Jesus" more than ever before—all because of abiding. I never thought that was possible. I never thought I'd be sitting in traffic thinking about Jesus and the things of God. But it happens, more often than ten-year-old me being forced to pray in the back seat of the car could have ever imagined.

And I love it.

That may sound kind of boring. *There are so many other fun things to think about than Jesus.* Sure, maybe? Depending on how you define *fun*, I guess. But those things can't give you the peace I've found. They can't give you the joy I've found. They can't give you the relief I've found. And they can't give you the stability I've found. All because of consistent and intentional abiding—the act of "making my home in Jesus."

That's not a "Look at how holy I am" brag. It's a "Holy crap, can you believe this?!"*

In the end, we're all devoted to something. We're all worshiping something. We're all abiding in something. "We will make our home somewhere," Comer says. "The question is 'Where?'"⁶

But how, Jon? How do you get to that point? How do you abide like you're talking about? What does it actually look like?

I'm glad you asked.

How Do You Do It?

This is going to sound overly simple, but I'm not being trite. The best way to learn how to abide is to start abiding. It's to do it. It's to practice it. It's to try and fail, and then keep trying, and then keep failing. And then do it all over again.

The essence of abiding is conversation and communion with God. And the heart of communication with God is prayer. The best resource on prayer I've ever encountered is a book called *A Praying Life* by Paul Miller. I read it years ago, and it laid the foundation for my current abiding. If you feel stuck, consider these words from Miller:

---

* Trust me, there are some old friends and family members reading this right now, going, "Who is this guy?"

> Don't try to get the prayer right; just tell God where you are and what's on your mind. That's what little children do. They come as they are, runny noses and all. Like the disciples, they just say what is on their minds.[7]

How do you eat an elephant? As the saying goes, "One bite at a time." And that really does apply here.

My "bites" look like this: Every morning, I start out by turning on soft worship music and journaling a short prayer. I try to start by being thankful. "Father, thank you for _____." Maybe it's for something specific, like a recent encouraging conversation with a friend, or maybe it's for something general, like my family. I then move on to requests. "Father, please _____." Maybe that's a request for something for myself, my wife, or my kids. I also might add something I'm frustrated about. I've written some very angry and confused words directed *at* God. And, in fact, some of my most important realizations have come from venting sessions with the Father.

Finally, I ask two questions that Winship introduced me to in *Living Fearless* that have transformed my abiding time:

> "Father, what do you want me to know today?"
> "Father, what do you want me to do today?"

And then I listen. I'm still. Sometimes I close my eyes. Sometimes I sing along to the music. Whatever comes to mind during that time I write down. No matter how blunt, how wild, or how scary. That's one way God speaks to me, and often that's how I know it's him: It's not something I would say. Then I meditate on his answers. From there, I'll often read something out of my Bible or a devotional. And if anything comes to me while doing that, I write it down.*

---

* For me, the journaling part is important. It helps me solidify my thoughts, it helps me remember them, and it helps me memorialize what God is doing in my life.

How long does this take? It depends. Some days it's thirty minutes. Some days it goes on for over an hour. I know, that sounds weird. Not long ago it would have sounded weird to me. But now it's just normal. So when do I know when to stop? I stop whenever I feel like God has released me to go about my day.

And it has transformed my life.

I don't know what your abiding time should look like. That's between you and God. Maybe start where I did and see what happens. Or start by simply reading God's Word and journaling. Sometimes I literally just open the Bible, see where it lands, read, follow the cross-references, and write. And if it lasts five to ten minutes, that's OK. Or maybe yours will look like a morning walk or an afternoon guitar session or getting on your knees. I don't know. For Heather Kopp, it looked like a lot of "nothing":

> I felt God inviting me to try something new and—for me—pretty radical. Something so hard that for a long time I couldn't manage to do it for more than five minutes a day. *Nothing*. God was inviting me to sit in my chair every morning with a candle and be still. Just be. Just listen. Just open my heart and stop trying to control my mind. For just a few minutes every day, stop trying to think my way out of this.[8]

And it transformed *her* life. She wasn't the greatest at it at first. But she got better. And eventually, abiding in her own special way with Christ gave her freedom, peace, and what she actually craved more than alcohol: "Sitting still was teaching me that when I think I'm thirsty for a drink, what I really crave is grace, and what I need most of all in the world is God."[9]

I love how Winship compares learning to abide to tuning our spiritual radios to the right frequency:

> Being able to hear God is a new skill. It's like learning how to understand Morse code. You have to practice; it's a discipline. Or it's like tuning in to a radio frequency. You turn the knob but there

are so many voices and so much static and noise. Then, finally, you find the station with the voice you recognize. The frequency resonates with your heart, and you keep fine-tuning it until the voice is crystal clear. You learn to hear God's voice above all other voices.[10]

Whatever your abiding will look like, the most important thing is just to start. It doesn't have to be perfect. Let it be what it is. And then let it become what it will become. One of the devil's greatest tools is to make you think you have to abide perfectly to abide at all. To pray perfectly to pray at all. You know why he does that? Because he's scared of you simply starting. Somewhere. Anywhere.

As Comer says, it will be hard, but that doesn't last forever:

> Should you pursue this, the early days of "practicing the presence of God" will likely be difficult and humbling, yet joyful—difficult because we *all* forget God constantly and get sucked back into hurry; humbling for the same reason, but full of joy and happiness as we begin to tap into the deepest ache of our souls: the desire for God. Over time, the wiring of your brain will begin to change, to heal from its rupture from your maker. New neural pathways will form. The more you pray, the more you *think* to pray. What first felt almost impossible eventually will become as easy and natural as breathing.[11]

Can you give five minutes to start? Just five minutes. I know it may feel awkward at first. It may feel hard. I felt that. But I promise you, it *will* change you. I'm reminded of the words of the modern-day monk Thomas Keating. He taught a form of abiding called contemplative prayer. Someone once said to him, "Oh, Father Thomas, I'm such a failure at this prayer. In twenty minutes I've had ten thousand thoughts!"

His response? "How lovely. Ten thousand opportunities to return to God."[12]

That's the attitude we should bring into our abiding time. It's not about perfection; it's about practice. It's not about a set of rules;

it's about a relationship. It's not about an obligation; it's about an invitation.

And it's not me who's inviting you to do it. It's God.

What Happens When We Abide

So, what does abiding do for us? C. S. Lewis said Jesus is the light by which we see everything else, and I can't think of a better analogy for what happens when we practice abiding with Christ.[13] It illuminates everything because he illuminates everything. And I mean everything.

I'm not just talking about our faults, although it does that. I'm not just talking about our path forward, although it does that too. What I mean is that it is the key that unlocks everything else in our lives. I'm not saying this in some sort of prosperity gospel way where we turn God into a genie. I'm saying it in the way that it is foundational to our entire life. Not just our sobriety or our relationship with alcohol.

Want more faith, more trust, and more peace? Abide.

Want practical ways to reorder your life? Abide.

Want to experience godly grief? Abide.

Want to surrender? Abide.

Want to want God more than you want alcohol? Abide.

Want new desires? Abide.

Want to stop trying to escape? Abide.

Want clarity? Abide.

Want direction in your life? Abide.

Want reconciliation? Abide.

"You see, a person doesn't learn to abide," Winship explains. "A person abides and then learns what happens as a result of abiding."[14] And don't think you have to have it all together to abide either. You abide so that you can start putting it all together. Or back together.

What I found as a result of abiding is more than I could have ever imagined. Yes, I found sobriety. But I found so much more. I continue to find so much more. And I dare you to test it out and see what you find as well.

TEN

Finding Your True Identity (Step 2)

> The journey in discovering your true identity in the kingdom of God is an eternal journey. There is no end to the depths of who God made you to be.
>
> —Jamie Winship, *Living Fearless*

I wasn't even a full month removed from my last drink.

Brett and I were out to dinner with another couple from our church. The wife happened to be in the mental health field and had recommended my therapist, Gina, to me. That suggestion was obviously a good one. So when she recommended a book, I perked up. She talked about how this book had challenged her, encouraged her, and even changed her. Her husband said the same thing.

High praise, I thought.

Desperate for growth and change, I unlocked my phone and purchased the digital version while we were still talking. During that period of my sobriety journey, I found myself open to nearly any suggestion. If it had the slightest chance of helping me leave who I was behind, I'd try it. I think that's part of the humility that repentance breeds (and needs).

As Brett retreated into the bedroom to lie down when we got home, I grabbed my e-reader and began a journey I didn't realize would change my life. As soon as I started, I couldn't stop. Before I realized it, I was halfway done. I forced myself to go to bed, then picked it back up in the morning. By week's end I had finished. It gave me a new perspective. It gave me new insights. It affirmed old ideas that I had written off or buried. It unlocked mysteries.

And it gave me a new identity.

Yes, a new identity. An identity that was partially already there but that I had allowed the devil to obscure and skew. An identity that would lead to the book you're reading now. An identity that will shape the rest of my life. An identity that turbocharged not only my sobriety but, more importantly, my relationship with Christ.

The book that I'm talking about is one I've already introduced. It's *Living Fearless* by Jamie Winship. We talked about Winship last chapter regarding abiding, but his real focus is on identity. And his book is the best resource I've found on the topic.

While I could quote it endlessly, that doesn't make for a great experience. So I'll limit my recounting of what he says to the essentials. But in the end, you should just read the book in its entirety.

Why? Because I believe with everything inside me that if you want to not just survive but thrive, not just run away but run toward something, not just be but become, then you have to find your identity. Not your general identity, but your specific one—the specific one given to you by the Creator of the universe. Once you start living out of *that* identity, life becomes about so much more than just drinking or not drinking, more than just counting days of sobriety, and more than just what you *can't* do.

You are awakened to a sense of calling, urgency, and even creativity that you have never experienced before. You become defined not just by what you've done or what you do but by who you truly are. And the shackles that have held you back become the experiences that propel you forward.

Do you want that? If so, keep reading.

What Is Identity?

I'm a big fan of defining terms. I think there's a lot of confusion (and arguments) because we don't take the basic step of making sure we're on the same page. It's why the first rule of debate club (unlike fight club) is to define your terms. So I'm going to define *identity*. That may seem simple, but I think the word is deeper and richer than we realize, especially if you're a Christian.

I don't pretend this is *the* definition. But as I've wrestled with my own identity and let Jesus invade every aspect of my life, it's been a helpful definition. And I think it's more complete than what you'll find in any dictionary too.

So here it is: *Identity is who you are—including your characteristics, your purpose, and your calling—as defined and given by God.*

How does that feel? Maybe read it again and sit with it for a second before I unpack each aspect.

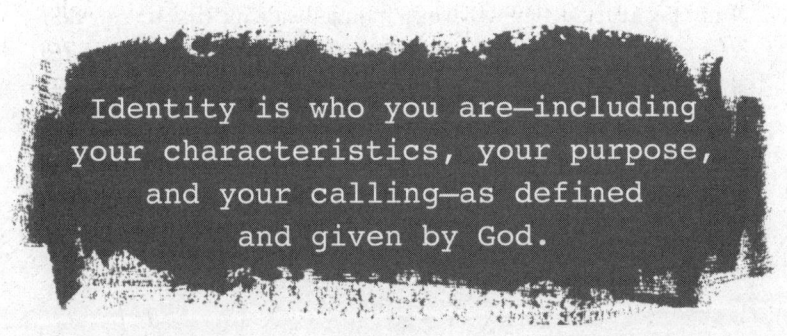

> Identity is who you are—including your characteristics, your purpose, and your calling—as defined and given by God.

Characteristics

Characteristics are maybe the most concrete of the three aspects. These include your physical attributes as well as your personality. They're your propensity to be introverted or extroverted. They're your body type. They're your skills, talents, and abilities. The things you can do well. We've noticed my son is expressive and fast, while my daughter is contemplative and deeply empathetic. Those are their characteristics given to them by God.

David describes this in Psalm 139:13–15:

> *For you formed my inward parts;*
>   you *knitted me together in my mother's womb.*
> I praise you, for I am fearfully and wonderfully made.
> Wonderful are your works;
>   my soul knows it very well.
> *My frame was not hidden from you,*
> when I was being made in secret,
>   *intricately woven* in the depths of the earth.
>   (emphasis added)

God has gifted you with characteristics that he "formed" and "knitted together," and they are "intricately woven" by, and "not hidden" from, him.

Purpose

I know other people define *purpose* granularly, but I see purpose as our general marching orders. A soldier's purpose, for example, is found in their oath that, among other things, they will "support and defend the Constitution of the United States against all enemies, foreign and domestic."[1] Similarly, John Piper—referencing the Westminster Catechism—explains that our general purpose is "to glorify God and enjoy him forever."[2]

In other words, as a Christian your general purpose—which, in a sense, is your general identity—is to be a child of God.

"Accepting and embracing your general identity as a child of God and believing it in your gut is the first step in recognizing your true worth," Matt Chandler explains. "Everything else about you and how God sees you, designed you, and has placed you today hinges on your understanding that you are made in His image and appointed an heir to His kingdom."[3]

Calling

Calling is where we get much more specific. Calling is that thing that burns within you. The thing you were meant to do with the rest of your life. The thing that makes you feel fulfilled. The thing that just feels (and is) right. The thing that God has told you to do and that everything else just seems to point to. To use the soldier analogy again, your calling is your specific duty and even more so your specific mission.

All three of these things—characteristics, purpose, and calling—combine to form my own identity. What is that? I'm a bold, courageous, decisive, and vulnerable storyteller. That's the identity God has given me. It's what I can't help but do. It's what gives me so much meaning. And when I'm operating in that identity, I feel the most alive!

For example, when I'm writing—when I'm "in the zone"—it's almost a spiritual experience. I'm engaging my mind, my body, and my soul in what I was created to do. Hours can go by and feel like minutes. I look forward to it. It's not something I *have* to do; it's something I *get* to do.

We'll go through how to find your own identity in a bit, but know this: It's both possible and essential that you find yours.

Why Your True Identity Is Essential

When I say identity is essential, I don't think I can overstate that. Your identity—as given by God—defines you. It's the standard by which everything else can be judged. For example, how can you make the best decision about your work if you don't know what you've been called to do? Certainly you can make *a* decision, but *a* decision is not necessarily the *best* decision. Think about what knowing each part of your identity outlined above could do to and for your life:

- Would understanding your unique characteristics lead to more flourishing?
- Would living within your general purpose give you a greater sense of belonging?
- Would knowing exactly what you're supposed to be doing give you a better sense of direction?
- Would embracing who you are help you say yes to the right things and no to the wrong ones?
- Would having your identity locked down help you get unstuck?
- Would being who you are meant to be give you more freedom and allow you to tear down idols in your life?

The answer to all of those questions is a resounding "Yes!"

And that's why your ultimate enemy, Satan, is working overtime to thwart your identity. He does not want you, under any circumstances, to know and especially embrace your true identity because of what it means for you and for the kingdom of God.

But he's sneaky.

See, the devil doesn't always try to outright block you from receiving your identity (although he does do that). Instead, one of his most devious and successful tactics is to get you living out of a false identity. Or, said another way, getting you to live out *part* of your identity but not the entire thing. By doing that, you're left floundering.*

---

* Winship explains there are two other tactics Satan uses: (1) to completely blind you to your identity, and (2) to get you to hate it or look down on it (*Living Fearless*, 127).

Think of it this way: A Navy captain called to control a mighty battleship is no threat when he accepts the opportunity to pilot a lowly tugboat and trawls aimlessly, chasing random radar blips. To be effective, he must go back to base and seize the full might of his rightful vessel and get clear and direct intelligence on how to defeat the enemy.

In the first scenario, the captain is living out *part* of his identity. He's controlling a ship, after all. But he's not living it out *fully*, and the enemy is perfectly happy with that.

Consider this: In Matthew 3, Jesus receives his identity from the Father while being baptized. Do you know what happens in Matthew 4? Jesus goes into the wilderness where he is tempted by the devil, and those temptations are all based on Jesus's *identity*. The devil keeps trying to get Jesus to accept cheap knockoffs of who he really is!

For most of my life, I was living only partially out of my full identity. I knew I was called to be a storyteller. In fact, I remember the first time that became obvious to me: I was in my preteen years, maybe eleven or twelve, and my family was taking a winter carriage ride. I asked the driver if I could sit by her because I loved horses. For the entire ride, we talked while I asked her questions. By the end, I knew her life story.

"I don't know why I'm telling you this, young man," I remember her saying.

After, my mom commented on my ability to make people comfortable and draw stories out of them. My soul smiled. I just knew I was created to do that.

The enemy knew that too.

How did my identity play out for most of my life, then? Sure, I was telling stories. I was in the news business, after all. But I was anything but bold, courageous, decisive, and vulnerable. Remember back to some of the stories I told you earlier. I was worried, I was nervous, I was anxious. I was on edge. I was defensive. And when I lived in *that* identity, I felt like I had to drink to keep those feelings even somewhat at bay.

Yes, I was telling stories. But I wasn't doing it out of my full and true identity. And I suffered because of it. I can only imagine how pleased my enemy was.

Winship explains this in terms of his own identity, which he describes as "militant peacemaker."* During one season, that looked like being a police officer, while in another it looked like being an overseas missionary:

> When I pick a vocation in that identity, I'm really, really good at it.... Conversely, if I pick a vocation outside of that identity, I'm going to be unhappy and frustrated and I'm not going to be good at it. Every day, I'm going to know I'm not good at it, and it's going to be bad. I can go to church and I can pray, but it's not going to make it better because I was not made to do whatever it is I'm doing outside of my identity.[4]

By the way, the problem wasn't in the stories I was telling when I was in the news business. It wasn't necessarily even in the industry in which I was telling them. I transitioned to a Christian nonprofit to tell stories, and even though it was better, I still struggled with many of the issues that plagued me. The issue was in *how* I was telling stories and, more so, who and what I saw myself as while I was telling them. I was timid, scared, confused, and defensive. I lacked a trust in and deep connection with God (i.e., abiding).†

---

* As he explains in the *Living Fearless Guided Journal*, though, that identity has now matured into "untier of knots."

† That said, I recently turned down a lucrative offer to return to the news industry. The general job aligned with my identity, but the specific duties would have been grueling, the expectations unrealistic, and I would have been miserable again. This is key: Your identity gives you a better picture of what you can do, but just because you *can* do something doesn't mean you should do it. Not every opportunity within your identity is a good idea. You still need to weigh all the factors.

I was living in an incomplete, and thus false, version of my identity. And that led me to chase escapes, believe Satan's lies, and look for fulfillment elsewhere. For example, when I wasn't operating in the "bold, courageous, decisive, and vulnerable" aspect of my identity I struggled with imposter syndrome. I felt unprepared. I felt incapable. And most importantly, I felt unworthy. Guess what: That's a false identity.

"'I am unworthy' is an identity statement, and when I live my life according to this identity, it's painful. This is the false me," Winship explains.[5]

By the way, where did that unworthiness start for me? It started with trauma at a young age that began speaking a false identity to me. I felt unseen. I felt unprotected. I felt abandoned. And thus, it told me I was unworthy.

So, what was a crucial part of me finding my true identity? Uncomfortable but necessary therapy aimed at rooting out the core issues and lies that I had believed my whole life, and the binge drinking that became the easy way to silence those lies.

Can you see how this is all starting to fit together?

Friend, you need to find your true identity. Until you do, you are missing out on so much. Winship says it much more eloquently:

> You cannot know God in any deep way from a false identity. You just can't. Satan's desire, whether you believe in Satan or not, is that you live your life making guesses, mostly wrong, about who you are, who God is, and who your neighbor is. You end up guessing your way through life and doing the best you can. That's one way to live—most people do it that way—but it's not a great way to live. You might survive with this strategy, but you will not thrive.[6]

How to Find Your True Identity

Now it's time to find your true identity. I'll summarize the basics as I've gleaned them from Winship, but he provides the intricacies, details the caveats, and even troubleshoots if you're not hearing anything from God. (Hint: It has to do with anger and unforgiveness.) This process can take an hour, or it can take a year. And both are OK.

But know this: "We do not find our true self by seeking it. Rather, we find it by seeking God."[7] That's why it is so important to start with, and practice, abiding.

Step 1: Identify False Identities

Before you can ever embrace your true identity, you must gain power over your false identity. And like Dr. Alison Cook showed us earlier, you do that by naming it.

"Our false identity is a trash pile that invites wrong belief in a myriad of lies. Trying to eliminate every lie we believe is time consuming and difficult," Winship helpfully explains. "What is more effective is eliminating the false identity that attracts the lies and allows Satan a foothold into our spiritual life."[8]

Whether you realize it or not, if you're struggling with a misordered/disordered relationship, you're operating out of a false identity or even identities (plural). To name them, quiet your mind, invite Jesus into wherever you are, and then ask him to reveal your false identities. Listen. Write down the first thing that comes to mind. See, many times we are subconsciously aware of these false identities because the Holy Spirit is at work within us. Do this as many times as a new false identity comes to mind. Afterward, include when you think each false identity seemed to emerge and what caused you to believe it.

Hint: The goal is to get to the root, not just the fruit. Try to go as deep as possible.

Step 2: Ask for Your True Identity

I know, this step may seem too easy, but "you do not have, because you do not ask" (James 4:2). I don't think my sanctification story would be as messy if I had learned how to practice better communication with God earlier in my life and actually asked him for things—especially good things that align with who he is.

So, once again, say a prayer. Quiet your mind and ask God to reveal your true identity—what *he* calls you, how *he* sees you, and who *he* says you are. Consider the lies and false identities you identified earlier and ask him to reveal the *truth*. Then listen. *Really* listen. When it comes to your true identity, a lot of us have an inkling. Remember, one of Satan's most successful tactics is to get you living in a perversion of your true identity. He twists it ever so slightly. Because of that, many of us have flirted with our true identity before. One important distinction here: Your identity is not your occupation. That's a way you live out your identity, but that's not who you are. That's what you do.

Jon, how will I know it's God speaking? That's a really important question. And Winship has a really important answer:

> You will know it's God speaking because whatever it is you sense from the Holy Spirit will be encouraging, it will align with Scripture, and it won't involve accusation or condemnation. And, whatever you hear, think, or sense from the Holy Spirit should resonate with you.[9]

Then there's this wisdom:

> God will only call you a name he would call himself. That's another way you know it's from God. He names us after himself, like a good father does. He'll call you something that moves you forward in freedom. It's something that excites you, brings you joy and peace. Sometimes what God says about us is almost too beautiful to believe.[10]

When I first heard "bold, courageous, decisive storyteller" (and later "vulnerable"), I started crying. I just knew that was it.

Dr. Cook calls this name giving (and name receiving) a "holy reframe." I think that's an absolutely beautiful term. When God gives you your identity, he reframes the hurt, the pain, and the mess. He reframes *you*. Dr. Cook uses the story of Jacob in the Bible (see Gen. 32) to make the point. See, Jacob's past was messy. He had tricked his father and scammed his brother. In fact, his name actually meant "deceiver." However, after he physically and literally wrestled with God by the Jabbok River, he was given a new name, a new identity: Israel.

"It accounted for all of who Jacob had become, not just who he had been," Dr. Cook explains. "He was no longer a mere trickster. . . . He'd grown and changed."[11]

Friend, no matter what you've done, God does not define you by it. He has a new name—a new identity—waiting for you. "A holy reframe" of all that's happened, no matter how dirty or messy.

That's why what we call ourselves matters. I just can't accept that I'm only "Jon the alcoholic" for the rest of my life. No, I'm "Jon the bold, courageous, decisive, and vulnerable storyteller" who has a story of recovery. I've undergone a holy reframe.

You can too.

Step 3: Look for Confirmation

This may seem a little confusing at first, but while your identity is personal, it is not private.

Think about that for a second. Your identity is not something that's meant to be hidden. It's not something that is meant only for you, even. What God gives to us he tells us to give to others (see Luke 6:30–37).

That also means something else: Your identity will be affirmed and confirmed by others, especially in the context of biblical community. It can't not be. Winship explains why:

> Scripturally speaking, true identity is received from God in community through the intuitive mind in prayer. The counterfeit of Christ-centered identity is radical individualism. Radical individualism is self-generated and subjective and leads only to internal and external conflict. Contrarily, true identity is the essence of who you are, gifted to you by God and meant to be discovered in relationship with him. It's the "I" you carry deep inside of you . . . secured in love, value, and worth. Your unique and true identity is meant to bless the world.[12]

Friend, I can't stress this enough: You are not meant to be a lone ranger. Not only do we all have blind spots that we need others to reveal (see Prov. 12:15; Gal. 6:1–5), we are also told to call out what is good and encourage one another (see 1 Thess. 5:11; Heb. 10:24–25).

If it's true that your identity is God-given, then it must be true that it's to be used to fulfill his good works (see 1 Cor. 12:12–27; Eph. 2:10). And if it's true that it is being used to fulfill his good works, then it is true that others can't help but see it and call it out (see Matt. 5:14–16).

I'm going to go out on a limb and say that if you are living in healthy, biblical community and others don't seem to be affirming your identity, you need to seek God fervently about whether you are living in a false identity instead.* You're missing out and suffering needlessly if you don't.†

Don't Absorb Someone Else's Identity

Even once you get your identity, there's still a learning curve. You still have to practice living it out. And one of the temptations is to try and absorb someone else's identity.

---

* That's not to say that when you're living in your true identity you won't face opposition. You will. Maybe even from those you love. But if you're being thwarted at every turn, spend time with God and ask him to reveal if there's been a misunderstanding. He'll let you know.

† And if you're struggling to hear anything, check your heart for unforgiveness and unresolved anger. Winship covers this extensively in part three of his book.

I remember exactly where I was when God made that clear to me. I was sitting by an afternoon campfire while on vacation, trying to make a video for social media about a devotion idea. But no matter how many times I tried—probably ten times—it just wasn't turning out.

I finally gave up.

That's when God spoke to me, "Jon, your identity is lived out through your writing. I gave this idea to you so you would write it, not film it. That's your skill and calling. Stop trying to co-opt someone else's identity."

That was a sobering moment.

See, I think it's a real challenge for a lot of us not to look around and want what other people have. That's especially hard in the age of social media. We see people doing incredible things, and we think, *Why not me?*

We want their abilities.

We want their talents.

We want their influence.

We want their platform.

We want their followers.

We want their likes.

We want their reach.

We want their things.

We want their job.

We want their life.

We want, we want, we want . . .

And while we're trying to absorb *their* identity, we're missing out on the incredible flourishing and contentment that come from living in *our* identity!

Friend, I'm not created—you're not created—to be someone else. God has given you unique gifts, unique talents, unique abilities. He's given you a unique identity. When you pursue what others have instead of Jesus, you miss out on what he has for *you*. You miss out on joy and fulfillment. You miss out on him. And all of *us* miss out too. Because when you're operating in your true identity, you (and it) can't help but bless others. Let me say this as emphatically as I can: Stop depriving the world of what God has put inside you!

"There are ideas inside your mind, heart, and spirit that no one has ever thought of before. And the beauty is that these ideas want to come out of you," Winship explains.[13] Press into that instead of trying to absorb someone else's identity.

"The enemy likes it very much when we try to be a knockoff of other people rather than growing into the people God has designed us to be," Chandler explains, recounting how he fell into a similar trap. "But the fact is, we don't need more of the same. The world needs faithful, committed followers of Jesus who are brave and bold enough to live and serve as their authentic, God-crafted selves."[14]

There are some incredible things waiting for you when you embrace who God has created you to be. When you know who you really are, you stop settling for false versions of yourself that lead to escapism. You stop trying to numb. We numb when we can't stand our reality. And living in our true, God-given identity is the most comforting form of reality there is.

So, are you brave and bold enough to find and live in your authentic self?

ELEVEN

Practicing Radical Vulnerability (Step 3)

> Confessing to one another is the greatest way to form true community because it draws people together.
>
> —Jamie Winship, *Living Fearless*

Confession time. Now that I'm sober, one of my new guilty pleasures is watching hoof-trimming videos. Yes, hoof-trimming videos. (It's amazing what happens when you stop drinking.)

If you don't know what I'm talking about, these videos follow trimmers and farriers as they manicure and repair infected livestock feet. YouTube put one of these videos in my feed once, and I was instantly hooked.

One of my favorite trimmers on the internet is a Scottish man with an amazing sense of humor. He doesn't hold back from showing you the sometimes graphic nature of his business.

As I've watched his videos, I've been struck by what happens time and time again. After noticing a limping cow, he restrains it and begins examining its feet. From there, he begins grinding off the outside of the "hoof horn" until he finds a crack. Once he finds one, he uses a very sharp and focused knife to remove smaller layers of keratin. And then, without fail, the small crack leads to a massive cavity underneath, filled with dirt, manure, and painful infection that, if not treated, can kill the cow. He then continues cutting away, exposing the infected area before cleaning it out and applying disinfectant.

Talk about a metaphor for our own lives!

Guess what: You and I have cracks—small fissures of the soul that serve as entry points for the dirt and manure of life. If we don't expose those cracks, if we don't dig out the junk that gets stuck in there and treat the underlying infection, it breeds greater spiritual disease that can eventually kill us. That's especially true when you consider this: So many times, a hoof trimmer sees the tiniest of cracks that to you and me would look like nothing. But his experience tells him to start cutting away to get to the root problem.

Are you limping? Chances are you have small cracks in your life. Are you willing to do what it takes to treat the infection inside? It needs to be exposed and cleaned. We have to let in the disinfectant that Jesus offers. If we don't, it could kill us.

So how do we do that? We expose the infection through radical vulnerability.

In chapter 6, we talked about the importance of vulnerability to combat shame. But vulnerability is a prescription that treats many ailments—including our misordered/disordered relationships and our traumas.

That's made clear in the Bible, for starters. Remember, true confession is a key aspect of vulnerability, and we see throughout Scripture the power of that practice (see James 5:16; 1 John 1:9). I especially love how Proverbs 28:13 puts it: "Whoever conceals his transgressions will not prosper, but he who confesses and forsakes them will obtain mercy." You can't be any more clear about the power of exposing our struggles.

But it's not just about confessing what we've *done*. That's only part of being radically vulnerable. The truth is many of us were victims before we were perpetrators.* That's why it's important to expose to the light what's been done *to* us so there can be full healing. Brené Brown explains the research:

> In a pioneering study, [researchers] studied what happened when trauma survivors . . . kept their experiences secret. The research team found that the act of not discussing a traumatic event or confiding it to another person could be more damaging than the actual event. Conversely, when people shared their stories and experiences, their physical health improved, their doctor's visits decreased, and they showed significant decreases in their stress hormones.[1]

I know it may not seem like it, but opening up about our darkest secrets is both spiritually and scientifically proven to be good for us.

Why Vulnerability Has to Be Radical

However, there's a problem. As we covered in chapter 8, we've gotten used to regular vulnerability. Our sinful natures know how to skirt around it. They know how to fake it. They know how to outsmart it. That's why we need radical vulnerability.

Let me give you a detailed example.

I've sat in a lot of men's groups where we go around the circle and every guy talks about their "struggle with lust." We live in a pornified world, after all. In the last twenty years, nearly every man I've met has struggled with it, and the rest are probably lying.

---

* That's not an excuse for evil or evil people. But it is a helpful explanation for what tends to be true.

But in these men's groups, the guy who I *know* is watching porn weekly or even daily simply owns up to a "lust issue." In other words, he confesses to a lesser sin in order to mask the bigger issue. He hides behind regular vulnerability and appeases his conscience: *See, I admitted it. They know.* And then he goes on doing what he's been doing for years because he's convinced himself and others that he's "battling it."

If that man were radically vulnerable (if he practiced true confession), he would describe exactly what's going on: how many times he's doing it, the tricks he's used to hide it, and the lies he's told to defend it. Why doesn't he? Because that type of vulnerability and confession truly brings his issue to the light where it can be killed. But he doesn't want that. He wants to assuage his conscience while still holding on to his sin. It's what counselor and author Chuck DeGroat calls "fauxnerability."[2]

I did that. All throughout my misordered/disordered slide, we were active members of our church and even led a small group. But I wasn't being radically vulnerable. I was holding back. I was giving just enough to make it seem like I was OK.

This line from Matt Chandler should hit us hard: "I've seen that to be 99 percent known is to be unknown."[3]

It reminds me of one of my favorite stories from C. S. Lewis and his masterpiece work of fiction *The Great Divorce*. In this allegory, he tells the story of someone who presents with a sly pet lizard on his shoulder. The lizard torments the man despite the man's pleas for it to be quiet. Eventually, an angel offers to take care of the lizard, and the man agrees. But when the angel goes to kill the animal, the man bristles, afraid that the process will be too painful.

"Honestly, I don't think there's the slightest necessity for that," the man says. "I'm sure I shall be able to keep it in order now. I think the gradual process would be far better than killing it."

Practicing Radical Vulnerability (Step 3)

The lizard eventually pipes up, trying to convince the man that he can keep him (the lizard) in check, even apologizing for getting out of hand at times.

"And I'll be so good," says the lizard. "I admit I've sometimes gone too far in the past, but I promise I won't do it again."*

Not surprisingly, then, the man yells, "Get back!" when the angel first tries to kill the lizard. "You're burning me. How can I tell you to kill it? You'd kill *me* if you did."

"It is not so," the angel responds.

"Why, you're hurting me now."

"I never said it wouldn't hurt you," the angel says wisely. "I said it wouldn't kill you."

The man finally relents but cries out to God for help. And after the angel kills the lizard, some incredible things happen: The man is physically transformed, and he gains power over the lizard, which is also transformed into a horse that transports the man to new heights and allows him to scale "impossible steeps."[4]

What a perfect picture of the difference between regular vulnerability and radical vulnerability. Regular vulnerability is a man (or woman) who is annoyed and knows he needs help, but doesn't want to go through the painful process of killing what torments him. Radical vulnerability is a man (or woman) who is willing to do whatever it takes to kill his struggle, cries out to God for help, realizes his true identity, and then takes dominion over that struggle and uses it to propel him to new heights.

Can you see why the devil hates radical vulnerability, then? He wants us to keep our sins, our struggles, our issues in the dark. He wants them to fester and infect us. So he lies to us. He tells us that exposing what's really going on will be too painful. Guess

---

* By the way, doesn't this sound exactly like our misordered/disordered drinking?

what: It *is* painful, but it's never *too* painful. It's never as painful as what's waiting for us if we don't expose it. Sure, it's not fun. But that discomfort helps save you from disintegration.

Another thing the devil says is that radical vulnerability is actually weakness. What a crock! Vulnerability is courage. Brown puts it this way: "Vulnerability sounds like truth and feels like courage. Truth and courage aren't always comfortable, but they're never weakness."[5]

No, vulnerability *strengthens* our souls. How? Because when we are fully known—the beautiful *and* the ugly parts—we find peace and relief. How many times have you felt that way after getting something off your chest, whether good or bad? You felt that way because exposing ourselves and laying ourselves bare is the pathway to finding true freedom.

You know who knew this well? Paul. The man who persecuted Christians "to the death" never held back on exposing his past.* He was always talking about how horrible he was. He was radically vulnerable about it. And instead of ruining his ministry, it actually *became* his ministry (see 2 Cor. 12:9).

He's not alone, though. The apostle Matthew did the same thing, as Brennan Manning points out:

> It is interesting that whenever the evangelists Mark, Luke, or John mention the apostles, they call the author of the first Gospel either Levi or Matthew. But in his own Gospel, he always refers to himself as "Matthew the publican," never wanting to forget who he was and always wanting to remember how low Jesus stooped to pick him up.[6]

So where do you start when it comes to practicing radical vulnerability? Well, I'm not asking you to post your deepest, darkest struggles and traumas on social media. No, the best way to start

---

* See Acts 22 and Galatians 1.

practicing radical vulnerability is to go one degree more vulnerable than you think you should in whatever context you're currently practicing it, either with a friend, a loved one, or in a group.

Just one degree.

Whenever you're sharing, ask yourself, *What would it look like to share just a little more? What would it look like to go one degree more vulnerable?* And then do that.

It's going to be uncomfortable, but it's going to be beautiful. And before you know it, you'll find yourself riding off to new heights after having been transformed, just like the man in Lewis's story.

The Importance of Community

There's an implied understanding when it comes to radical vulnerability, but I want to make sure to call it out. It's the idea that vulnerability in many senses requires community. You should be honest and vulnerable with yourself, you should be honest and vulnerable with God, but you really need to be honest and vulnerable with others.

Simply put, you need to practice radical vulnerability in the context of community. We see this throughout the Bible. Jesus carried out his ministry with a close-knit group of twelve friends while traveling among a plethora of even more disciples. Additionally, the New Testament is littered with calls to be in community (see Heb. 10:24–25; James 5:16). It's what the researchers say too. "The vulnerability journey is not the kind of journey we can make alone," Brown explains.

But what is the best type of community for practicing radical vulnerability? Will just any do? Well, consider this: Brown says two of the most important elements for healthy community are trust and safety.[7] Where do we see those best playing out?

There's only one place I know that can deliver them on a consistent basis: *biblical* community. Why? Because for those who follow him, God is ultimately the safest person in the universe! And a community founded on him, his words, and his commands gives us the building blocks for building trust and being vulnerable. Consider the following:

- We're taught to love and serve one another (see 1 Pet. 4:8–10).
- We're taught to sacrifice (see John 15:12–13).
- We're taught to be compassionate, kind, humble, meek, and patient (see Col. 3:12).
- We're taught to forgive (see Col. 3:13).
- We're taught to turn the other cheek (see Matt. 5:38–42).
- We're taught not to withhold kindness (see Job 6:14).
- We're taught to honor our friends over ourselves (see Rom. 12:10).
- We're taught to be present in times of adversity (see Prov. 17:17).

I could go on and on, but you get the point. The commands of the Bible—the teachings of Jesus—can't help but build trust and make us feel safe. The community built around those teachings, then, has to be the best and safest place to practice radical vulnerability.*

That's not to say that every biblical community is great at this. I actually think the church in general can do better at teaching and fostering radical vulnerability. Remember, Christians have historically loved stories of salvation but struggled or gone silent when it comes to stories of messy sanctification. But just because we need to work at fostering and accepting radical vulnerability doesn't mean we haven't been given the best tools to implement it.

---

* For a practical, real-world example of how this has played out in my own biblical community, visit ChristianAlcoholic.com and download the free bonus material.

Some of you have undoubtedly experienced deep church hurt. Leaders (and others) have harmed you, physically, emotionally, or spiritually. There's been abuse. There's been manipulation. And I am truly sorry for that. But what I'm saying is that the problem isn't with the commands of Jesus; the problem is with how they've been lived out.

"Regardless of the times in which you live, the church is both beautiful and a giant mess. The church is a place of deep healing and sometimes deep hurt," Chandler reminds us. "People have found lifelong, deep friendships built on grace and kindness, and they've been betrayed in ways that are hard to recover from."[8]

And yet, "Don't let the enemy deceive you into believing the church is your enemy. She's a mess at times, but she's beautiful too."[9]

Don't Settle

But if biblical community is the best version of community, the worst type is community that swaps true connection for counterfeit connection. And today, technology is leading to a host of counterfeit connections.

I'm not saying that technology has no purpose. I think it's wonderful that you can find fellow travelers—and strugglers—on the road to glory by simply googling whatever your issue is. But online communities and tools are a supplement, not a substitute.

Pastor and nonprofit leader Chris Harper puts it so well: "Technology is giving us the illusion of friendship without any of the hard work (or actual benefits)."[10]

While I'm not some old man shouting at the sky, I think the mandate to continue to meet together in Hebrews 10:24–25 is best lived out in actual, physical proximity overseen by and connected to a local church.* There are obvious exceptions for sickness and

---

* This assumes you're also regularly attending a local church and not just a small group. Corporate worship is important.

other outlying circumstances. But I do feel a strong conviction that biblical community is supposed to look like *actually* meeting face-to-face, *actually* bearing one another's burdens in a practical sense at times, and *actually* having to sacrifice time and put in effort. Culture is constantly looking for shortcuts. But "the Way" of Jesus has always been countercultural, and it values sacrifice and authentic connection.

Author and social scientist Johann Hari shocked the world in 2015 when he released a TED Talk in which he boldly declared, "Almost everything we think we know about addiction is wrong."[11] What do we get so wrong?

"The opposite of addiction is connection," he says.[12]

In his now-famous talk that has over twenty-one million views, he takes direct aim at our digital-first mindset:

> The connections we have or think we have are like a kind of parody of human connection. If you have a crisis in your life, you'll notice something: It won't be your Twitter followers who come to sit with you. It won't be your Facebook friends who help you turn it around. It'll be your flesh-and-blood friends who you have deep and nuanced and textured face-to-face relationships with.[13]

We were already headed there before 2020, but COVID accelerated it. Is it any wonder, then, that a pandemic that starved us of connection led to an increase in addiction-related "deaths of despair" in the United States?[14] George F. Koob, director of the National Institute on Alcohol Abuse and Alcoholism, reveals the shocking numbers: "During the first 2 years of the pandemic, the number of death certificates listing alcohol as a factor soared from 78,927 to 108,791—an increase of nearly 38%."[15]

And I think a big part of that is because we've quite literally made a deal with the devil when it comes to connection and technology.

We've traded showing up for logging on.

We've traded prayer requests for friend requests.

We've traded physical hugs for virtual likes.

We've traded community for convenience.

We've traded being known for being alone.

We've traded confession for comfort.

We have paid the price, and we continue to pay the price, for that deal. And it's time to stop settling.

"We ... must be deeply rooted in church communities," Tim Keller explains. "We have to avoid picking what we need here and there without ever becoming grafted into a cohesive community of other believers."[16]

It Doesn't End There

OK, so maybe you see the need for radical vulnerability. You even understand that biblical community is the best means to live that out. Great. But your journey doesn't—it can't—end there.

For starters, while confession and radical vulnerability should be practiced within biblical community, it's not necessarily confined to biblical community. For example, part of my practicing radical vulnerability looked like being open and honest with my therapist. Is my therapist a Christian? Yes. But she isn't a part of my biblical community in the traditional sense. And yet, she was an essential part of my step 3.

Your own implementation of this step should be practiced among biblical community, but in addition, it can be practiced in a therapist's office, an online group, a twelve-step program, or with your significant other.

That last one is important. I've seen some guys be eager to tell their men's group what they're struggling with and then hide it from their wives—sometimes for years. That's not only being dishonest with someone else, but it's also being dishonest with yourself because you're believing the lie that full confession isn't really necessary. Will it sometimes take time to build up the courage for full confession as the Holy Spirit works on you? Yes. But you know when you're dragging your feet.

Second, confession, or even telling your story, is not the end goal of radical vulnerability. Healing is. I've seen some people be open about telling their stories as a way to excuse their actions, skirt accountability, or lower the expectations of growth in their lives. Don't do that. Name your struggles and what has led to them, but then grow from them. Take action.

In the end, "confession" without change is just a more dressed-up way to assuage your conscience. It isn't healthy and it's incomplete. Remember, repentance requires action. And action, not coincidentally, brings us to our final step: obedience.

TWELVE

Obeying What God Tells You to Do (Step 4)

> God's grace calls you to submit. But it offers you true freedom like you've never known before.
>
> —Paul David Tripp, *New Morning Mercies*

Obedience. That's a dirty word in culture today, right? In fact, some of you may have just cringed a little bit. And I get it.

I've been a part of faith traditions, denominations, and churches that have abused the word *obedience*—especially when it comes to faith. Do whatever the slick preacher tells you to do, usually involving some sort of monetary "seed of faith," and then God will bless *that* obedience. And so, for a long time I was the one cringing when I heard the word. But in my journey to return to Jesus and fillet myself open to him, I've found a freedom in obedience that has transformed my life and my thinking.

I think (actually, I know) it could change you too.

Just as we're all abiding in something (see chapter 9), we're all obedient to something because we're all worshiping something. We were built to worship, but sin changed the object of that worship. The decision, then, isn't *whether* we will obey; it's what or whom we are going to obey. The best option, since it is the option we were created for, is to obey God. Even Jesus "learned" obedience (Heb. 5:8). So when we do that, we're like a perfectly-tuned violin joining Beethoven's symphony.[*]

In the most basic sense, obedience is doing what God tells us to do. You "hear" it, you do it.

But how do I hear what God is saying to me? That's probably the most common question I get when it comes to obedience. We've covered the answer in a couple places (see chapters 9 and 10), but let me bring it all together. And really it comes down to one word: *abiding*. We hear God when we spend time with him. (Shocker.) It's not necessarily like an audible voice, although that can happen. So many times he speaks to us while we're reading (and through) Scripture, praying, singing, or journaling. In those times, I've found the voice of God "sounds" like my voice in my head, but it says things I wouldn't normally say. Many times it goes against what's easy and what I want to do. It can even be a strong, counterintuitive urging. That brings me to the final point (and this is important): No matter what the voice sounds like, whatever you hear *must* align with Scripture. If it doesn't, then there's a problem.[†]

OK, so now that we know how to hear God (although I'm not pretending it doesn't take practice), when we *do* hear him, it's our responsibility to actually do what he says. Easier said than done, I

---

[*] See John Piper's sermon explaining how we were created for worship here: https://www.desiringgod.org/messages/worship-god--2.

[†] I also recommend having a godly friend, adviser, or advisers to "test" what you believe God is telling you.

get it. Growing up, I bristled at doing what God said because his commands were manipulated by faith leaders around me. But after attending the abiding retreat in Georgia and being encouraged to press into the idea of obedience there, I learned of its true beauty and power. I realized it was time to go all in. To really embrace it. Especially since Scriptures like Psalm 112:1, Luke 6:46, John 14:15, 1 Peter 1:14, and 1 John 5:3 make clear that obedience is an essential part of following Jesus. In fact, it's not optional; it's natural: When you abide in Jesus, you will obey, and when you obey Jesus, you will abide (see John 14:23).

So, not long into my sobriety journey, I finally committed to actually doing what God told me to do. I sought out what he was telling me in my abiding time and in Scripture, I said quick prayers throughout the day, and then I acted on what he told me. Like, really acted on it. Very practically.

If Scripture told me to do something, I did it.

If he told me to meet with someone, I met with them.

If he told me to send an email, I sent it.

If he told me to stop doing something, I stopped doing it.

If he told me to pray about something, I prayed about it.

And when he told me to write a book about the most painful, embarrassing, and vulnerable aspects of my life, I wrote it.

In addition, I began looking for ways to practice the general commands he outlines in his Word. Things like loving others, giving up idols, and of course, not getting drunk. Simply put, I took the words from John 14:15 seriously: "If you love me, you will keep my commandments."

Today, because of that obedience, my life both externally and internally looks very different. There's an inner peace that has led to external transformation. I'm seeing things happen in my life, even in my head, that I never thought possible.

That's because God's guidance is good. His discipline is desirable. His fences keep us free. Through commitment to Christ's words, through following them, we are transformed. And that obedience both changes us and shows others that we are changed. In fact, I've come to learn that the benefit of obedience is most often found in the simple *act* of being obedient, and is not at all about the outcome of what you're being told to do.

As you examine your relationship with alcohol, and if the Holy Spirit makes clear that you have a misordered/disordered relationship with it, no doubt there are going to be those around you curious about whether a change has actually occurred. In fact, *you* might be wondering that as well. Here's the simple way to know: Look for evidence of obedience. I'm not just talking about obedience in relation to alcohol. Remember, you can cut back on drinking or even stop drinking and still have a misordered/disordered relationship with alcohol. I did. Instead, look for *other* evidence of obedience. It will be there.

I want that for you. So let's walk through the finer points of obedience together, the final step to breaking free.

Obedience Requires Sacrifice

You can't really talk about obedience without talking about sacrifice.

In the Bible, we see obedience and sacrifice go hand in hand. They're different sides of the same coin. To be obedient, then, will require sacrifice. It did for Jesus, and it will for us (see Phil. 2:8).

"To follow Jesus will require you to leave something behind," John Mark Comer writes. "Following Jesus *always* requires you to leave something behind."[1]

Obeying What God Tells You to Do (Step 4)

He continues:

> Within the heart of a true disciple is a settled intention of the will to obey Jesus. As unpopular as the idea of obedience is in the modern era, Jesus *assumes* that his disciples will obey his teaching. Because that's the *very nature* of discipleship: learning "to obey everything [Jesus has] commanded you."[2]

That's the heart of Luke 9:23–27 as well. We are to "deny [ourselves] and take up [our] cross daily" to follow Jesus (v. 23). But are we willing to deny ourselves *fully*, not just when it's easy or comfortable?

My favorite example of this from the Bible is in 1 Chronicles 21. It's an absolutely beautiful and mind-blowing example of what happens when we practice obedience and sacrifice.

In the passage, we find that King David has (once again) been disobedient. As a result, God sends a "pestilence" to strike the land of Israel, leading David to repent. That's when an angel tells David to go to a specific person's property and offer a sacrifice. When David arrives, the landowner is awestruck. So awestruck, in fact, that he offers the land and animals to David for *free*. A nice deal if you can get it, right?

Wrong.

See, it wasn't enough to just obey—David realized he needed to sacrifice too. And not just in the sense of offering an animal. His obedience needed to be costly as well.

So instead of taking the man's offer, David says, "No, but I will buy them for the full price. I will not take for the Lord what is yours, nor offer burnt offerings that cost me nothing" (v. 24). What a statement! He can't and won't sacrifice that which costs him nothing.

Friend, when God tells us to do something, that something will require sacrifice. Maybe not money but pride, fear, or comfort.

225

> When God tells us to do something, that something will require sacrifice.

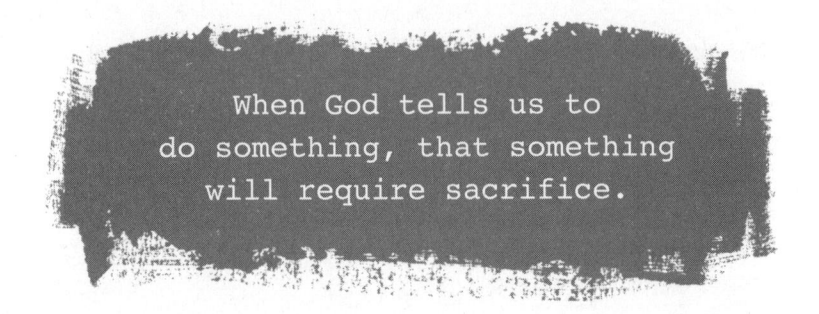

And here's the key point: Sacrifice has to be costly. Quite literally, the definition of sacrifice is that it costs you something.

That's already an incredible lesson. But it gets better.

As the 1 Chronicles 21 story wraps up, chapter 22 starts out with something that brings me to tears every time. It's one little verse that appears like an "Oh, by the way," but it's crucial to the rest of the biblical narrative. Here it is: "Then David said, 'Here shall be the house of the Lord God and here the altar of burnt offering for Israel'" (v. 1).

That little area that David refused to take for free? That random property that God told David to go to? That act of obedience that was costly? It became the site of the temple, the greatest and most important building in the history of Israel. The most sacred and glorious reflection of God on earth in the Old Testament.

Friend, when we are obedient—and when it costs us—he turns it into something beyond what we could ever imagine.

So let me ask you: What will God build with your costly obedience?

If we're honest with ourselves, a lot of times we treat our faith like we're at a garage sale, don't we? We see the price tag, and then we try to negotiate the cost down. We know what our faith calls us to do, and yet we want to haggle our way out of it.

But Jon, God's gift of salvation is free!

Yes, God's gift of salvation *is* free. There's nothing we can do to earn it. And yet, when we accept that free gift, there is something that we're called to do. We're called to be obedient. To sacrifice. That obedience and sacrifice is not to earn the free gift, but it is rather out of gratitude for what's already been given. It's not a requirement; it's a response.

Think of it this way: There is nothing we can do to earn right standing with God. But once we experience that right standing through what Jesus did on the cross, we are compelled to follow his commands and sacrifice. Not out of duty but out of love.

"We do not live God's way in order to become His children, but out of gratitude that we are already God's children," Tim Keller writes.[3]

Obedience is both required and chosen. Mandatory and voluntary. Commanded and offered. The great German theologian Dietrich Bonhoeffer describes this as cheap grace versus costly grace.

"Cheap grace is the preaching of forgiveness without requiring repentance, baptism without church discipline, Communion without confession, absolution without personal confession," he says. "Cheap grace is grace without discipleship, grace without the cross, grace without Jesus Christ, living and incarnate."[4]

On the contrary, costly grace "is the kingly rule of Christ, for whose sake a man will pluck out the eye which causes him to stumble; it is the call of Jesus Christ at which the disciple leaves his nets and follows him."[5]

Maybe you're here right now and you're thinking, *OK, I hear all this, and I'm willing to cut back on my drinking. I see it's become misordered/disordered.* And yet, what if God's not calling you to cut back? What if he's actually calling you to give it up? I can't tell you how many times I took God's call for me to completely stop drinking, filtered it through my own desires, and ended up just "cutting back." And where did that get me? Wading in my own crap (figuratively and quite literally) in the ocean.

Friend, we know that getting drunk is a sin. But that's not the only standard we have when it comes to sin and drinking. In the end, doing *anything* you know you shouldn't, or not doing something you know you should, is sin as well. Remember, James 4:17 makes that clear.

My point is this: If the Holy Spirit is telling you to be obedient in a very specific way in relation to your drinking—even if you're not getting drunk—and you don't do that, it's not enough. Is that a high standard? To the world, yes. But not to the Christian. That's the call.*

This type of obedience may seem like a boring life to you. I get it. For *years* I couldn't imagine myself without alcohol. Not just because my body craved it but because I couldn't imagine having fun, coping, or functioning without it. And yet, God wasn't trying to *steal* pleasure from me; he was trying to give me *greater*, *healthier*, *truer* pleasure—pleasures forevermore (Ps. 16:11)! We need to grow beyond the idea that God's commands are meant to make us miserable or steal our joy. It's the exact opposite.

I really cannot hammer this point home enough: The pleasure, joy, fulfillment, and satisfaction that I have found as a result of being obedient to Jesus is something I have never experienced before. The peace I have now truly surpasses understanding. And I'm not some monk. I'm a sports-loving, Netflix-watching, meme-liking, pickup-truck-driving guy who has found freedom and transformation in being obedient to Jesus.

"True freedom is not found in doing whatever you want to do whenever you want to do it," Paul David Tripp says. "True freedom is never found in putting yourself in the middle of your world and making it all about you. True freedom is not found in resisting the

---

* However, I get that sometimes, because of withdrawal symptoms, giving up drinking can't only look like quitting cold turkey.

call to submit to any authority but your own.... When you attempt to do these things, you never enjoy freedom; you only end up in another form of bondage."[6]

Oh, how true I have unfortunately found that to be. And the story of humanity is littered with painful examples of others who have had to learn that lesson as well. But there is another way. In God's upside-down world (which is really right side up), peace, freedom, and relief are found in obedience to the person who knit everything together, the person who knows how we are wired and how this world is supposed to work. Isn't that good news? It's like taking your broken Model A to Henry Ford himself to be fixed. You'd do whatever he says, wouldn't you? We make awful soul mechanics. Awful gods too. So does alcohol. The best mechanic and the best god is the true God.

"We were created to live in willing submission to [God's] will for us," Tripp concludes. "Hence . . . freedom is found in the willing submission of our hearts to his authority."[7]

I know that type of obedience may be hard to imagine right now when you can't even get through a day without your glass of wine, your bourbon, or your beer. It may be hard to see a life where facing your emotions or the realities of the day—buying a house, parenting your children, dealing with work, walking through that illness—without something to "take the edge off" seems impossible. But I'm telling you, it's possible. And there's something greater waiting for you on the other side.

It's hard as hell, but it's as sweet as heaven. Because it's a taste of it.

The Final Ingredient

There's one final truth about obedience, though. It's more of a key ingredient, you could say. It's what breeds obedience. It's how you get to the point of sending bold emails you never thought you'd send because God told you to. It's this: trust. Unless you trust Jesus, you will consistently find it hard to obey him.

When you trust God, it's pretty incredible what you find yourself doing for him. When I talk about trust, though, it's not just a general thing. You have to trust specifically that . . .

- he loves you
- he knows you
- he knows what's best for you
- he's going to come through
- he's good
- he's enough
- he cares
- he hears you
- he will protect you
- he will provide
- he will not abandon you
- he did not make a mistake

There are others. Think of your root issues that have led you to any of your misordered/disordered relationships and then think of the lies they've drilled into you. For me, those last four are very particular to the lies I grew up believing and that fueled my drinking. So when I started trusting that Jesus would protect me, provide for me, not abandon me, and did not make a mistake in creating me the way he did, my obedience to him became something I got to do, not something I had to do.

In the end, obedience is not about a set of rules. It's not about behavior modification. It's not about empty rituals. It's about responding to the relationship that you're cultivating and *experiencing*. When you begin falling in love with Jesus again (or for the first time), you begin trusting him. And when you trust, you obey. You do what he says and what he's called you to do. You take whatever steps you need to. However small. Not begrudgingly—although sometimes skeptically, for sure.

And where does all *that* start? With abiding. By being with Jesus.

Do that, make your home *in* him, and one day you'll look back and realize you're farther down the road than you ever imagined you could be. You'll smile. Not because of what you have done but because of what he has done and what he is doing. You'll realize—maybe suddenly, maybe slowly—your messy sanctification isn't a liability but a weapon. And you've become, as Brennan Manning says so beautifully, the type of person the world desperately needs: "someone daring enough to be different, humble enough to make mistakes, wild enough to be burned in the fire of love, [and] real enough to make others see how phony we are."[8]

That's a life of peace and fulfillment. Of flourishing. And it's a life that only Jesus can provide. Welcome. Or maybe, welcome back.

Epilogue

"Go in the Strength You Have"

I grew up on an old farm in Wisconsin. It wasn't a working farm, but it still had the barns and the silo. And while I only had a horse, there were some summers I would help in the milking parlor when I went to spend time with my cousins.

My point is that I'm well acquainted with farm culture. I know how farmers look, how they smell, and how they're viewed. And even though we can romanticize them, the truth is, they are not appreciated enough.

That's just one of the aspects that makes the biblical story of Gideon so amazing. His has become one of my favorites. It's the story of a lowly farmer who is constantly doubting God, has no special skills, but leads a revolution. And it's the perfect story for you and for me: the alcoholics, the addicts, the disordered drinkers, the fakes, the frauds, the floundering, the philanderers, the imposters, and the all-around messy and sanctified.

Give me just a minute to explain.

Epilogue

We pick up Gideon's story in Judges 6 as he's threshing wheat, which means he's separating the grain from the stalk. But he's doing it in a winepress. Why? Because he's trying to stay out of sight of the Midianites, Israel's enemy at the time.

In other words, he's literally farming in fear. He's hiding.

So imagine the look on Gideon's face when an angel shows up and tells him that he's been chosen to lead Israel's army. In fact, the angel says something quite strange. He doesn't refer to Gideon by his name but rather refers to him by a new title: "mighty warrior" (v. 12 NIV).

Not surprisingly, the man who's literally hiding from the enemy is confused. He says, no way. He goes on to make all sorts of excuses. He tries to convince God that he's a nobody. He's unqualified. He's small and weak.

"Look at me. My clan's the weakest in Manasseh and I'm the runt of the litter" he says. (v. 15 MSG). *Find someone else!*

God doesn't. In fact, the angel utters some simple but incredible words: "Go in the strength you have" (v. 14 NIV).

After a little more arguing, and after Gideon asks for numerous signs just to make sure God's got the right guy, Gideon eventually obeys. But then God pulls an audible: He tells Gideon he has to whittle down his army from thirty-two thousand men to just three hundred. Gideon obeys again, and those three hundred men go on to defeat the entire army of Midian.

So how does a scared, hiding farmer become a "mighty warrior" who defeats an entire army with only 0.9375 percent of the men he started with? And why am I telling you this story? The answer is the same: Because Gideon followed the exact four steps I have outlined in this book.* Let me show you.

---

* Remember, I don't claim to have invented these. They are not "my" steps.

Epilogue

Step 1: Gideon abides with God. God sends an angel, and Gideon entertains God's messenger, spends time with him, and converses with him.

Step 2: God gives Gideon a new identity. It's a stunning development because it's so different from the identity he has been operating out of. Gideon goes from scared farmer to "mighty warrior."

Step 3: Gideon is radically vulnerable. At first, it may seem disrespectful that Gideon tries to make excuses and talk himself out of the job, but it's actually crucial. By being honest, Gideon is actually building trust with God, and God uses that to empower Gideon.

Step 4: Gideon obeys. God first tells Gideon to "go in the strength you have," and he does it. And then when God tells him to whittle down the men so that God's ultimate power will be more evident, Gideon obeys again. It doesn't make sense, but he does it anyway.

Gideon abides, he receives and lives out a new identity, he's radically vulnerable, and he obeys. And what happens after he does those four things? He's victorious, and Israel experiences freedom.

Friend, I know that you may feel like Gideon right now as you consider whether you have a misordered/disordered relationship with alcohol and what God might be telling you to do with that. You're scared, you're hiding, and you may even feel small and weak. I felt all those things. I doubted that there was anything *but* those things waiting for me in life. My drinking had clouded both my physical and spiritual eyes.

But guess what: Like Gideon, I am a mighty warrior. *You* are a mighty warrior. It's part of the general identity we've all been given as children of God. How do I know? Because only warriors are given armor (see Eph. 6:10–18).

Epilogue

You have been given armor and are called to fight this battle. Go fight it! I know it may seem like you don't have much to give, but God is saying, "Go in the strength you have." And he's going to take care of the rest.

Listen, I'm not telling you to do something I didn't do myself. I know what it's like. I didn't have much strength on the beach in Miami that night with Brett. But with the little I had, I sent an email. I made a commitment. I took a step. I was one degree more vulnerable. And despite the odds—despite the family history, cravings, and trauma—stacked against me, I'm here now, writing these words to you, telling you that freedom is possible. I know it because I've experienced it.

God's got you. I've given you the example. I've given you the steps. He's given you the power. Now "go in the strength you have." And don't be surprised at what happens when you do.

You may not slay an army, but you will slay some dragons.

Acknowledgments

Acknowledgments can be boring. I get it. So if you're reading this, I applaud you. *But* they are important. So many people help make a project like this a reality, and to not recognize them just feels like a crime. So that's what I'm going to do.

Thank you . . .

To the **readers** of my blog at TheVeritasDaily.com. You were some of the first people to see versions and tidbits of these words as I worked out my messy sanctification story in fear and trembling. Thank you for the likes, comments, shares, subscriptions, and especially prayers.

To the **elders at Providence Church in Frisco, Texas**. You wrapped your arms around me when I was so broken, cared for me and my family, and loved us so well.

To **Sarah Matzke**. You thought I was helping you on your book, but you were really helping me on mine. Thank you for modeling radical vulnerability.

To my agent, **Tom Dean**, at A Drop of Ink. You took a chance on me and this idea and have been championing it from the beginning.

Acknowledgments

That is not lost on me. Your calls, texts, and encouragements have been life-giving.

To my PR rep, **Kristin Cole**, at KC Communications. You were the second person I sent this idea to. I thought for sure you were going to tell me it was too toxic, too raw, and too taboo. Especially for the Christian world. You didn't. Instead, you confirmed how needed it was.

To **Caroline Beidler** and the recovery writers group, including **Ericka Andersen, Dr. Lee Warren, Christy Osborne, Dr. Zoe Shaw, Jenn Kautsch, Christina Dent, Laura Smith, Lisa Stanton,** and **Heather Kopp**. The early support and the feedback all of you gave were invaluable. Caroline, your help in navigating sobriety and the recovery community, as well as your continued reassurance that what I wanted to say was important, can't be overstated.

To my editors, **Rachel McRae** and **Kristin Adkinson**, as well as the entire team at **Revell** and **Baker Publishing Group**. From the moment we first met, Rachel, I knew you were the right person to oversee this project. Your genuine care and love for helping people are evident, not just professionally but personally. Thank you for answering my questions, dealing with my over-the-limit manuscript, and pointing me in so many right directions. What do you say we do another one soon?

To **Tanner Stevenson**. I can't say enough what our friendship means to me and how God has used you to call me to himself—and continues to do so.

To my mentor, **Steve French**. If not for your act of service and obedience in May 2023, we would have never gone on the retreat in Georgia that set the stage for this transformation. Your continued support and mentorship—as well as your trust and confidence in me—have reminded me that no one is ever too far gone for God's grace.

Acknowledgments

To **Brett's family** for not heaping shame and condemnation on me when you could have. I know what I've shared here and privately is not easy to hear. But you have exemplified what the church needs to be when it comes to loving people with messy sanctification stories.

To **my family**, especially my **mom**, for allowing me the freedom to share my story. God has brought us through so much, and he's redeeming all the hurt and pain. For our good and his glory.

To **Gina Carter**, for having such care and compassion as I wrestled with so much in your counseling office. There's a reason I can't stop referring people to you.

And finally, to **Brett**. I can't put into words how your love has pointed me to Jesus, even when it didn't seem like it was working. You are the most kind, compassionate, long-suffering, beautiful person I know. This period has brought us closer together than I ever could have imagined, and I am so thankful for it. For you. I love you.

More Resources

For more resources, including a bonus chapter, resource guide, video roundtable, daily email, and the special companion podcast, visit ChristianAlcoholic.com.

BONUS CONTENT

Get exclusive bonus material!

christianalcoholic.com

Notes

Introduction: Blitzed on the Beach

1. *New Oxford American Dictionary*, 3rd ed. (2015), under "sanctification."

Chapter 2 Am I an Alcoholic?

1. Substance Abuse and Mental Health Services Administration, "Impact of the *DSM-IV* to *DSM-5* Changes on the National Survey on Drug Use and Health," June 2, 2016, https://www.ncbi.nlm.nih.gov/books/NBK519702.

2. See a more comprehensive list of withdrawal symptoms here: https://umem.org/files/uploads/1104212257_CIWA-Ar.pdf.

3. Erin Jean Warde, *Sober Spirituality: The Joy of a Mindful Relationship with Alcohol* (Brazos Press, 2023), 92.

4. Brennan Manning, *The Ragamuffin Gospel: Good News for the Bedraggled, Beat-Up, and Burnt Out* (Random House, 2005), 85, Kindle.

Chapter 3 A Slow Fade

1. Jamie Elmer, "Is Depression Contagious?," Healthline, May 23, 2018, https://www.healthline.com/health/is-depression-contagious.

2. Dr. Alison Cook, *I Shouldn't Feel This Way: Name What's Hard, Tame Your Guilt, and Transform Self-Sabotage into Brave Action* (Thomas Nelson, 2024), 82.

Chapter 4 How Does This Happen?

1. National Institute on Alcohol Abuse and Alcoholism, "Understanding Alcohol Use Disorder," September 2024, https://www.niaaa.nih.gov/publications/brochures-and-fact-sheets/understanding-alcohol-use-disorder.

2. National Institute on Alcohol Abuse and Alcoholism, "Risk Factors: Varied Vulnerability to Alcohol-Related Harm," accessed March 28, 2025, https://www.niaaa.nih.gov/health-professionals-communities/core-resource-on-alcohol/risk-factors-varied-vulnerability-alcohol-related-harm#pub-toc3.

Notes

3. Maik Dünnbier, "Beer and Booze Wars and Celebrities: How Super Bowl 2023 Turned into an Alcohol Advertising Frenzy," Movendi International, February 20, 2023, https://movendi.ngo/blog/2023/02/20/beer-and-booze-wars-and-celebrities-how-super-bowl-2023-turned-into-an-alcohol-advertising-frenzy-and-what-it-means-for-the-future/.

4. Celeste Yvonne, *It's Not About the Wine: The Loaded Truth Behind Mommy Wine Culture* (Broadleaf Books, 2023), 4.

5. "Holly Whitaker on Pursuing Sobriety in a Culture Obsessed with Drinking," Yahoo Life Videos, April 14, 2021, https://www.yahoo.com/lifestyle/holly-whitaker-pursuing-sobriety-culture-195634288.html?.

6. Annie Grace, *This Naked Mind: Control Alcohol, Find Freedom, Discover Happiness and Change Your Life* (Avery, 2018), xix, Kindle.

7. Collin Hansen, "Young, Restless, Reformed," *Christianity Today*, September 2006, https://www.christianitytoday.com/2006/09/young-restless-reformed/.

8. LifeWay Research, "Churchgoers Views–Alcohol," http://research.lifeway.com/wp-content/uploads/2018/11/American-Churchgoers-Alcohol-2017.pdf.

9. John MacArthur, "Beer, Bohemianism, and True Christian Liberty," Grace to You, August 9, 2011, https://www.gty.org/library/blog/B110809/beer-bohemianism-and-true-christian-liberty.

10. Ericka Andersen, "The Secret Sin of 'Mommy Juice,'" *Christianity Today*, April 22, 2024, https://www.christianitytoday.com/ct/2024/may-june/secret-sin-mommy-juice-women-alcoholism-wine-mom.html.

11. Warde, *Sober Spirituality*, 15.

12. Cook, *Shouldn't Feel This Way*, 81.

13. David Powlison, *How Does Sanctification Work?* (Crossway, 2017), 100.

14. Paul David Tripp, *New Morning Mercies: A Daily Gospel Devotional* (Crossway, 2014), October 4.

15. Heather Kopp, *Sober Mercies: How Love Caught Up with a Christian Drunk* (Jericho Books, 2014), 142–43, emphasis added.

16. Saint Gregory of Nyssa, quoted in John A. Coleman, "Post-Christmas Spiritual Reading," *America*, December 27, 2012, https://www.americamagazine.org/content/all-things/post-christmas-spiritual-reading.

17. Matt Chandler, *The Overcomers: God's Vision for You to Thrive in an Age of Anxiety and Outrage* (Thomas Nelson, 2024), 40, Kindle.

18. Charles Spurgeon, "Jotham's Peculiar Honor," The Spurgeon Center, October 24, 1907, https://www.spurgeon.org/resource-library/sermons/jothams-peculiar-honor/#flipbook/.

19. Manning, *Ragamuffin Gospel*, 30–31.

20. Manning, *Ragamuffin Gospel*, 25.

21. Henry Scougal, "How and How Not to Think About Religion," Crossway, June 2, 2022, https://www.crossway.org/articles/how-and-how-not-to-think-about-religion/.

22. Will Timmins, "What's Really Going On in Romans 7," The Gospel Coalition, July 2, 2018, https://www.thegospelcoalition.org/article/romans-7-apostle-paul-confession/.

23. John Mark Comer, *Practicing the Way: Be with Jesus. Become Like Him. Do as He Did.* (WaterBrook, 2024), 90.

24. Kopp, *Sober Mercies*, 201.

25. C. S. Lewis, quoted in Cook, *Shouldn't Feel This Way*, 34.

26. Chandler, *Overcomers*, 60–61.

Chapter 5 Root vs. Fruit

1. Debra Fileta (@debrafileta), Instagram post, April 10, 2024, https://www.instagram.com/p/C5lhGkhLGxO/?img_index=1.

2. "Epigenetics and Child Development: How Children's Experiences Affect Their Genes," Center on the Developing Child, Harvard University, https://developingchild.harvard.edu/resources/what-is-epigenetics-and-how-does-it-relate-to-child-development/.

3. Caroline Beidler, "Epigenetics and Recovery," *Circle of Chairs*, September 21, 2024, https://open.substack.com/pub/carolinebeidler/p/epigenetics-and-recovery.

4. John Calvin, quoted in Tony Reinke, "The Nail in the Coffin of Our Hearts," Desiring God, October 1, 2017, https://www.desiringgod.org/articles/the-nail-in-the-coffin-of-our-hearts.

5. Cook, *Shouldn't Feel This Way*, 100.

6. Cook, *Shouldn't Feel This Way*, 101.

7. Cook, *Shouldn't Feel This Way*, 113.

8. Timothy Keller, *Galatians for You*, God's Word for You (Good Book Company, 2013), 157, Kindle.

9. See Daniel J. Siegel and Tina Payne Bryson, *The Power of Showing Up: How Parental Presence Shapes Who Our Kids Become and How Their Brains Get Wired* (Ballantine Books, 2020).

10. Quoted in Chuck DeGroat, *Healing What's Within: Coming Home to Yourself—and to God—When You're Wounded, Weary, and Wandering* (Tyndale Refresh, 2024), 111, Kindle. This quote is also often attributed to Dr. Peter Levine.

11. Chandler, *Overcomers*, 14–15.

12. Aundi Kolber, "When Father's Day Hurts," aundikolber.com, June 18, 2015, https://aundikolber.com/2015-6-17-when-fathers-day-hurts/.

13. Chandler, *Overcomers*, 15–16.

14. Dr. Lee Warren, "I Am Not Just My Brain," *Self-Brain Surgery with Dr. Lee Warren*, September 15, 2024, https://open.substack.com/pub/drleewarren/p/i-am-not-just-my-brain.

15. Warren, "Not Just My Brain."

16. Cook, *Shouldn't Feel This Way*, 105.

Chapter 6 Combating Shame

1. Curt Thompson, *The Soul of Shame: Retelling the Stories We Believe About Ourselves* (InterVarsity Press, 2015), 13.

2. Brené Brown, *Daring Greatly: How the Courage to Be Vulnerable Transforms the Way We Live, Love, Parent, and Lead* (Avery, 2012), 68–69, Kindle.

3. Chandler, *Overcomers*, 17.

4. Manning, *Ragamuffin Gospel*, 117.

5. Brown discusses this idea in *Daring Greatly*, 71.

6. Brown, *Daring Greatly*, 73.

7. Brown, *Daring Greatly*, 74.

8. Thompson, *Soul of Shame*, 14.

9. John Piper, "The Good End of Godly Regret," Desiring God, December 30, 1984, https://www.desiringgod.org/messages/the-good-end-of-godly-regret.

10. John Bloom, "Two Kinds of Regret, One Kind of Hope," Desiring God, May 31, 2013, https://www.desiringgod.org/articles/two-kinds-of-regret-one-kind-of-hope.

11. Manning, *Ragamuffin Gospel*, 117.

12. Matt Chandler (@mattchandler74), Instagram post, March 27, 2024, https://www.instagram.com/p/C5B-2j7r0j1/.

13. Ian Simkins (@iansimkins), Instagram post, March 10, 2024, https://www.instagram.com/p/C4WvQF8MKhN/?img_index=4.

Chapter 7 Messy Sanctification

1. John Owen, *The Mortification of Sin* (Christian Focus, 1996), chap. 2, https://archive.org/details/mortificationofs00owen/page/28/mode/2up.

2. Andrew Davis, *The Power of Christian Contentment: Finding Deeper, Richer Christ-Centered Joy* (Baker Books, 2019), 197, Kindle.

3. Keller, *Galatians for You*, 170.

4. Manning, *Ragamuffin Gospel*, 30.

5. Powlison, *How Does Sanctification Work?*, 29–30.

6. Dietrich Bonhoeffer, *Life Together* (Harper & Row, 1954), 110.

7. Keller, *Galatians for You*, 25.

8. Paul Thomas Thigpen, "Eight Paths Toward Spiritual Fitness," Bible.org, May 29, 2011, https://bible.org/article/soul-building.

9. Chandler, *Overcomers*, 8.

10. Paul Carter, "Did King David Rape Bathsheba?," The Gospel Coalition, Canadian Edition, April 22, 2018, https://ca.thegospelcoalition.org/columns/ad-fontes/did-king-david-rape-bathsheba/.

11. Scott Sauls, "Can Christian Hypocrisy Be Overcome?," *The Scott Sauls Blog*, October 6, 2024, https://open.substack.com/pub/scottsauls/p/redeeming-the-black-eye-of-christian.

12. Chandler, *Overcomers*, 115.

13. Keller, *Galatians for You*, 27.

14. Manning, *Ragamuffin Gospel*, 28.

15. Tripp, *New Morning Mercies*, August 29.

16. Sonya VanderVeen Feddema, "A River of Gratitude," *Christian Courier*, December 22, 2021, https://www.christiancourier.ca/a-river-of-gratitude/.

17. Jamie Winship, *Living Fearless: Exchanging the Lies of the World for the Liberating Truth of God* (Revell, 2022), 49, Kindle.

18. Tripp, *New Morning Mercies*, October 1.

Chapter 8 Finding Sobriety

1. Mandy Erickson, "Alcoholics Anonymous Most Effective Path to Alcohol Abstinence," Stanford Medicine, March 11, 2020, https://med.stanford.edu/news/all-news/2020/03/alcoholics-anonymous-most-effective-path-to-alcohol-abstinence.html.

2. Tony Reinke, *Ask Pastor John: 750 Bible Answers to Life's Most Important Questions* (Crossway, 2024), 273–74.

3. Cook, *Shouldn't Feel This Way*, 105.

Chapter 9 Abiding in Christ (Step 1)

1. Winship, *Living Fearless*, 21.

2. John Piper, "What Does It Mean to 'Abide in Christ'?," Desiring God, September 22, 2017, https://www.desiringgod.org/interviews/what-does-it-mean-to-abide-in-christ.

3. Comer, *Practicing the Way*, 37.

4. Sinclair Ferguson, "What Does It Mean to 'Abide' in Christ?," Ligonier, March 6, 2020, https://www.ligonier.org/learn/articles/what-does-it-mean-abide-christ.

5. Comer, *Practicing the Way*, 41.

6. Comer, *Practicing the Way*, 38.

7. Paul E. Miller, *Beginning a Praying Life* (NavPress, 2013), 15.

8. Kopp, *Sober Mercies*, 145–46.

9. Kopp, *Sober Mercies*, 146.

10. Winship, *Living Fearless*, 127.

11. Comer, *Practicing the Way*, 45–46.

12. Cynthia Bourgeault, "The Method," Center for Action and Contemplation, February 13, 2017, https://cac.org/daily-meditations/the-method-2017-02-13/.

13. See C. S. Lewis, "They Asked for a Paper," in *Is Theology Poetry?* (Geoffrey Bless, 1962), 164–65.

14. Winship, *Living Fearless*, 230.

Chapter 10 Finding Your True Identity (Step 2)

1. "Oath of Enlistment," U.S. Army, https://www.army.mil/values/oath.html#.

2. John Piper, "What's the Origin of Desiring God's Slogan?," Desiring God, September 20, 2017, https://www.desiringgod.org/interviews/whats-the-origin-of-desiring-gods-slogan.

3. Chandler, *Overcomers*, 3.

4. Winship, *Living Fearless*, 29.

5. Winship, *Living Fearless*, 67.

6. Winship, *Living Fearless*, 99.

7. Winship, *Living Fearless*, 105.

8. Winship, *Living Fearless*, 85.

9. Winship, *Living Fearless*, 125.

10. Winship, *Living Fearless*, 127.

11. Cook, *Shouldn't Feel This Way*, 53.

12. Winship, *Living Fearless*, 117.

13. Winship, *Living Fearless*, 34.

14. Chandler, *Overcomers*, 9.

Chapter 11 Practicing Radical Vulnerability (Step 3)

1. Brown, *Daring Greatly*, 82.

2. Chuck DeGroat, "Vulnerability and Fauxnerability: Learning the Difference Is Essential for a Leader," *In All Things*, September 25, 2018, https://inallthings.org/vulnerability-and-fauxnerability-learning-the-difference-is-essential-for-a-leader/.

3. Chandler, *Overcomers*, 140.

4. C. S. Lewis, *The Great Divorce*, Collected Letters of C.S. Lewis (HarperCollins, 2009), 47–48, Kindle.

5. Brown, *Daring Greatly*, 37.

6. Manning, *Ragamuffin Gospel*, 143.

7. Brown, *Daring Greatly*, 47.

8. Chandler, *Overcomers*, 119.

9. Chandler, *Overcomers*, 121.

10. Chris Harper, "The Week in Review," *Good Trouble*, August 10, 2024, https://charper.substack.com/p/the-week-in-review-1c5.

11. Johann Hari, "Everything You Think You Know About Addiction Is Wrong," TED, June 2015, https://www.ted.com/talks/johann_hari_everything_you_think_you_know_about_addiction_is_wrong?subtitle=en.

12. Hari, "Everything You Think."

13. Hari, "Everything You Think."

14. C. Angus, C. Buckley, A. M. Tilstra, and J. B. Dowd, "Increases in 'Deaths of Despair' During the COVID-19 Pandemic in the United States and the United Kingdom," *Public Health* 218 (May 2023): 92–96, https://www.ncbi.nlm.nih.gov/pmc/articles/PMC9968617/.

15. "Risky Alcohol Use: An Epidemic Inside the COVID-19 Pandemic," National Institutes of Health, July 28, 2023, https://web.archive.org/web/20240827184621/https://covid19.nih.gov/news-and-stories/risky-drinking-alcohol-use-epidemic-inside-covid-19-pandemic.

16. Keller, *Galatians for You*, 30.

Chapter 12 Obeying What God Tells You to Do (Step 4)

1. Comer, *Practicing the Way*, 210.

2. Comer, *Practicing the Way*, 212.

3. Keller, *Galatians for You*, 33.

4. Dietrich Bonhoeffer, *The Cost of Discipleship*, First Touchstone Edition (Touchstone, 1995), 44–45.

5. Bonhoeffer, *Cost of Discipleship*, 45.

6. Tripp, *New Morning Mercies*, August 28.

7. Tripp, *New Morning Mercies*, August 28.

8. Manning, *Ragamuffin Gospel*, 177.

JONATHON M. SEIDL (JON) has been telling stories his whole life. In fact, he's written over ten thousand of them, first after helping start a successful news website and then as the editor in chief of the popular nonprofit I Am Second. He writes and speaks all across the country on the power of storytelling, radical vulnerability, faith, mental health, and addiction. His previous book on anxiety—*Finding Rest*—instantly became a national bestseller. He currently runs the popular daily devotional website The Veritas Daily (TheVeritasDaily.com), where he writes on faith, culture, and addiction, while also finishing his master's in theological studies from Southwestern Seminary (SWBTS). In addition, he consults businesses, leaders, influencers, and nonprofits on how to tell their stories through his company, The Veritas Network. Originally from Wisconsin, he lives in Frisco, Texas, with his wife, Brett, and their children, Annie and Jack. You can book Jon to speak by visiting JonSeidl.com.

CONNECT WITH JON

WEBSITE AND BOOKING:
JonSeidl.com

DAILY DEVOTIONALS:
TheVeritasDaily.com

PODCAST:
JonSeidl.com/podcasts

@JonathonMSeidl
@JonSeidl
@JonSeidl

A Note from the Publisher

Dear Reader,

Thank you for selecting a Revell book! We're so happy to be part of your life through this work.

Revell's mission is to publish books that offer hope and help for meeting life's challenges, and that bring comfort and inspiration. We know that the right words at the right time can make all the difference; it is our goal with every title to provide just the words you need.

We believe in building lasting relationships with readers, and we'd love to get to know you better. If you have any feedback, questions, or just want to chat about your experience reading this book, please email us directly at publisher@revellbooks.com. Your insights are incredibly important to us, and it would be our pleasure to hear how we can better serve you.

We look forward to hearing from you and having the chance to enhance your experience with Revell Books.

The Publishing Team at Revell Books
A Division of Baker Publishing Group
publisher@revellbooks.com

Revell